HEALING THROUGH ART

McGILL-QUEEN'S INDIGENOUS AND NORTHERN STUDIES
BRUCE G. TRIGGER, EDITOR

1 When the Whalers Were Up North
Inuit Memories from the Eastern Arctic
Dorothy Harley Eber

2 The Challenge of Arctic Shipping Science, Environmental Assessment, and Human Values
David L. VanderZwaag and Cynthia Lamson, Editors

3 Lost Harvests Prairie Indian Reserve Farmers and Government Policy
Sarah Carter

4 Native Liberty, Crown Sovereignty
The Existing Aboriginal Right of Self-Government in Canada
Bruce Clark

5 Unravelling the Franklin Mystery Inuit Testimony
David C. Woodman

6 Otter Skins, Boston Ships, and China Goods
The Maritime Fur Trade of the Northwest Coast, 1785–1841
James R. Gibson

7 From Wooden Ploughs to Welfare
The Story of the Western Reserves
Helen Buckley

8 In Business for Ourselves
Northern Entrepreneurs
Wanda A. Wuttunee

9 For an Amerindian Autohistory
An Essay on the Foundations of a Social Ethic
Georges E. Sioui

10 Strangers Among Us
David Woodman

11 When the North Was Red
Aboriginal Education in Soviet Siberia
Dennis A. Bartels and Alice L. Bartels

12 From Talking Chiefs to a Native Corporate Elite
The Birth of Class and Nationalism among Canadian Inuit
Marybelle Mitchell

13 Cold Comfort
My Love Affair with the Arctic
Graham W. Rowley

14 The True Spirit and Original Intent of Treaty 7
Treaty 7 Elders and Tribal Council with Walter Hildebrandt, Dorothy First Rider, and Sarah Carter

15 This Distant and Unsurveyed Country
A Woman's Winter at Baffin Island, 1857–1858
W. Gillies Ross

16 Images of Justice
Dorothy Harley Eber

17 Capturing Women
The Manipulation of Cultural Imagery in Canada's Prairie West
Sarah A. Carter

18 Social and Environmental Impacts of the James Bay Hydroelectric Project
Edited by James F. Hornig

19 Saqiyuq
Stories from the Lives of Three Inuit Women
Nancy Wachowich in collaboration with Apphia Agalakti Awa, Rhoda Kaukjak Katsak, and Sandra Pikujak Katsak

20 Justice in Paradise
Bruce Clark

21 Aboriginal Rights and Self-Government
The Canadian and Mexican Experience in North American Perspective
Edited by Curtis Cook and Juan D. Lindau

22 Harvest of Souls
The Jesuit Missions and Colonialism in North America, 1632–1650
Carole Blackburn

23 Bounty and Benevolence
A History of Saskatchewan Treaties
Arthur J. Ray, Jim Miller, and Frank Tough

24 The People of Denendeh
Ethnohistory of the Indians of Canada's Northwest Territories
June Helm

25 The *Marshall* Decision and Native Rights
Ken Coates

26 The Flying Tiger
Women Shamans and Storytellers of the Amur
Kira Van Deusen

27 Alone in Silence
European Women in the Canadian North before 1940
Barbara E. Kelcey

28 The Arctic Voyages of Martin Frobisher
An Elizabethan Adventure
Robert McGhee

29 Northern Experience and the Myths of Canadian Culture
Renée Hulan

30 The White Man's Gonna Getcha
The Colonial Challenge to the Crees in Quebec
Toby Morantz

31 The Heavens Are Changing
Nineteenth-Century Protestant Missions and Tsimshian Christianity
Susan Neylan

32 Arctic Migrants / Arctic Villagers
The Transformation of Inuit Settlement in the Central Arctic
David Damas

33 Arctic Justice
On Trial for Murder, Pond Inlet, 1923
Shelagh D. Grant

34 Eighteenth-Century Naturalists of Hudson Bay
Stuart Houston, Tim Ball, and Mary Houston

35 The American Empire and the Fourth World
Anthony J. Hall

36 Uqalurait
An Oral History of Nunavut
John Bennett and Susan Rowley

37 Living Rhythms
Lessons In Aboriginal Economic Resilience and Vision
Wanda Wuttunee

38 The Making of an Explorer
George Hubert Wilkins and the Canadian Arctic Expedition, 1913–1916
Stuart E. Jenness

39 Chee Chee
A Study of Aboriginal Suicide
Alvin Evans

40 Stange Thigns Done
Murder In Yukon History
Ken S. Coats and William R. Morrisson

41 Healing through Art
Ritualized Space and Cree Identity
Nadia Ferrara

Healing through Art

Ritualized Space and Cree Identity

NADIA FERRARA

McGill-Queen's University Press
Montreal & Kingston · London · Chicago

ISBN 978-0-7735-2721-8 (cloth)
ISBN 978-0-2280-2634-1 (paper)
ISBN 978-0-7735-7198-3 (ePDF)

Legal deposit second quarter 2004
Bibliothèque et Archives nationales du Québec

First paperback edition 2025

Printed in Canada on acid-free paper that is 100% ancient-forest-free, containing 100% sustainable, recycled fibre, and processed chlorine-free.

This book has been published with the help of a grant from the Canadian Federation for the Humanities and Social Sciences, through the Awards to Scholarly Publications Program, using funds provided by the Social Sciences and Humanities Research Council of Canada.

Funded by the Government of Canada | Financé par le gouvernement du Canada | Canada | Canada Council for the Arts | Conseil des arts du Canada

We acknowledge the support of the Canada Council for the Arts.

Nous remercions le Conseil des arts du Canada de son soutien.

McGill-Queen's University Press in Montreal is on land which long served as a site of meeting and exchange amongst Indigenous Peoples, including the Haudenosaunee and Anishinabeg nations. In Kingston it is situated on the territory of the Haudenosaunee and Anishinaabek. We acknowledge and thank the diverse Indigenous Peoples whose footsteps have marked these territories on which peoples of the world now gather.

Library and Archives Canada Cataloguing in Publication

Title: Healing through art: ritualized space and Cree identity / Nadia Ferrara.

Other titles: Ritualized space and Cree identity

Names: Ferrara, Nadia, 1967- author

Description: Series statement: McGill-Queen's Indigenous and northern studies; 41 | Paperback reprint. Originally published in hardcover in 2004. | Includes bibliographical references and index.

Identifiers: Canadiana 2025014882X | ISBN 9780228026341 (paper)

Subjects: LCSH: Art therapy—James Bay Region. | LCSH: Self-perception. | LCSH: Art therapy. | CSH: Cree—Mental health—James Bay Region. | CSH: Cree—Ethnic identity. | CSH: Cree—Psychology.

Classification: LCC E99.C88 F47 2025 | DDC 616.89/165608997323—dc23

This book was typeset by Dynagram inc. in 10/13 Palatino.

McGill-Queen's University Press
Suite 1720, 1010 Sherbrooke St West, Montreal, QC, H3A 2R7

Authorized safety representative in the EU: Mare Nostrum Group BV, Mauritskade 21D, 1091 GC Amsterdam, the Netherlands, gpsr@mare-nostrum.co.uk

Mikayla, I dedicate this to you.

Contents

Figures xi

Acknowledgments xiii

1 Introduction 3

2 The Crees in Quebec 14

3 Cree Styles of Communication 47

4 Cree Mythopoetic Thought 59

5 Ritualizing Space through Art Therapy 89

6 Conclusion: Art Therapy as an Interstice for the Cree Self 118

Notes 135

References 147

Index 163

Figures

1.1 Luke's first picture 5
1.2 Luke's heart painting 6
1.3 Luke's portrait of me (detail from his first picture) 6
2.1 Cree home 15
2.2 Goose break 19
2.3 Bush lifeways 35
2.4 The Old Ways vs the New Ways 37
4.1 Smoking goose meat 67
4.2 Tom's caribou 73
4.3 Tom's day spirit 74
4.4 Tom's night spirit 75
4.5 Luke's killing of the goose 77
4.6 Tom's rabbit and lynx 81
4.7 Tom's bush cabin 82
4.8 Tom's baseball drawing 85
4.9 Tom's Rocky Mountains 86
4.10 Tom's clay beaver 87
4.11 Tom's dream (drawing) 87
4.12 Tom's dream (painting) 88
5.1 UPAP no. 1: Free drawing 94
5.2 UPAP no. 2: Kinesthetic drawing 94
5.3 UPAP no. 3: Scribble 95
5.4 UPAP no. 4: Scribble 96
5.5 Luke's drawing of the two of us 99
5.6 Luke: The bush and art therapy 99
5.7 Tom's medicine wheel 103
5.8 Luke's clay coin 104

5.9 Tom's dragon 106
5.10 Tina's bush drawing 108
5.11 Tom's "Going Home" 110
5.12 Tom's wigwam 110
5.13 Luke's clay boat 111
6.1 Luke's Indian mask 127
6.2 Luke's heart drawing no. 1 132
6.3 Luke's heart drawing no. 2 133

Acknowledgments

Many people have contributed to the making of this book and I am deeply grateful to those named and unnamed. First, I would like to wholeheartedly thank the Cree people who have given me so much valuable insight not only into their ways of life but even more so on who they are as individuals. They willingly brought me into their homes, gatherings, and rituals. I have vivid memories of sipping hot tea while sitting around a fire in the bushcamp, listening to the sounds of nature, absorbing the Northern Lights. Together we experienced a myriad of emotions, through songs, laughter, and silence. When the elders and youth spoke, I listened and vice versa – they felt my presence and I theirs. Both my definition of respect and theirs coincide and characterize the foundation of our relationship. I am indebted to them in allowing me to share their personal narratives with my peers and colleagues, as well as allowing me to reproduce their artwork to give form to their narratives.

This book initially began as my doctoral dissertation, and so I would like to thank the faculty at the Department of Anthropology at Université de Montréal, especially Gilles Bibeau, who first showed an interest in my clinical work and believed in its potential to contribute to anthropology. I owe special debts to Rémi Savard, Mariella Pandolfi, Pierrette Thibault, John Leavitt, and Kevin Tuite, who all contributed in some way in the formulation of my research ideas throughout my doctoral studies. Wholehearted thanks to other colleagues including Toby Morantz, Colin Scott from McGill University, George Fulford at the University of Winnipeg, and Richard Preston at McMaster University, and Adrian Tanner at Memorial University, all of whom opened up more avenues for exploration.

Special thanks to Guy Lanoue, my doctoral thesis supervisor, who consistently provided me with critical and constructive feedback, adding much to this book's breadth and scope, not to mention its clarity in presentation of the material. Dr Lanoue's insights helped me enhance my skills as an ethnographer and a clinician. I thank him for encouraging me to move beyond my focus on the importance of art therapy among the Crees and open my eyes to art therapy as a vehicle used for expressions of the Cree self.

Many thanks to Aurèle Parisien, my editor at McGill-Queen's, for believing in the potential of this book. Rather than disregarding it or being threatened by its multidisciplinary and complex character, Aurèle embraced the book from the start. To Lesley Barry and Joan McGilvray, thank you for your copy-editing, which did so much to enhance the book. I would especially like to thank Diane Mann, Rose Marie Stano, and Cynthia Romanyk at McGill University, Department of Anthropology, for their constant support and friendship. Special thanks to my students at both Concordia and McGill Universities for their help in exploring some of my ideas in class discussions: their insights enriched many aspects of my ethnography. I further express my gratitude to my husband, Tony, who has always remained by my side, providing me with love and support as well as his own critique of my ideas. I thank my family for their unconditional love and encouragement; without it I could not have accomplished what I have thus far. I thank my precious daughter, Mikayla, for reminding me on a daily basis the importance of reflecting on my own self, including my strengths and weaknesses, and moreover, for reminding me that she is the miracle in my life.

HEALING THROUGH ART

1

Introduction

This study provides a comprehensive analysis of the nature of Cree patients' experiences in art therapy and shows how art therapy is a means of revealing contradictory and ambiguous tendencies in the construction of the modern Cree self. It explores the Cree notion of the composite self, which consists of the individual autonomous self, the self-in-nature, and the self-in-the-collectivity. The Cree self is reciprocally embedded in the individual, in nature (i.e. the bush), and in the collective (i.e. the community), and the source of tension and instability for many Cree patients usually lies in integrating this latter dimension with the others. Art therapy facilitates the process of creating a new self by deconstructing the old, redefining the components, and building a new, multivocal self.

My entrance into the Cree world began in 1989 with my first Cree patient, a nine-year-old boy whom I began seeing in individual art therapy while working as an intern at a residential treatment centre in Montreal. Art therapy is a human service profession that uses art media, the creative art process, and patient responses to his/her created products as reflections of the patient's development, abilities, concerns, and conflicts. Art therapy is founded on the belief that the creative process involved in the making of art is healing and life-enhancing (AATA 2001, 10). It is practised in mental health, rehabilitation, medical, educational, and forensic institutions. Art therapists are professionals trained in both art and psychotherapy. Psychotherapy is the foundation of art therapy but, unlike psychotherapy, the primary language of art therapy is non-verbal, which leads to verbal in the form of narratives related to the images created. The premise is that the images the client or patient produces open avenues for the identification and communication of feelings, a process facilitated by the therapist, who may guide the client in his/her self-reflection. Through the creation of spontaneous imagery, the client's qualities, strengths, weaknesses, and strengths are given form.

Luke (a pseudonym, like all names used here), who was hearing impaired, was brought to Montreal from his northern Quebec Cree community because there was no treatment centre or group home facility in the region. Cree community workers, teachers, and foster families had difficulty dealing with Luke's impulsive and aggressive behaviours. The agency's clinical assessment workers had initially evaluated Luke and noted his hyperactive tendencies and "inappropriate" social skills, such as his inability to respect the privacy of others. Luke was labeled a "block of ice," and "not at the feeling level." In other words, Luke was judged to be unable to express his emotions verbally. As a result, he was considered as having an inability to relate to his emotions. In the clinical assessment report, this child was described as a typical "emotionally stoic Indian." These conclusions were made by non-Native counsellors and psychiatrists with no apparent knowledge of Cree styles of communication and interaction patterns or of Cree definitions of the self. The report was written in light of Euro-Canadian psychological norms and ignored Cree views of the behaviours being assessed. Moreover, Luke's identity as a Cree, that is, in terms of how he identified himself in relation to his cultural group of reference, was dismissed.

When I began my internship at the residential treatment unit in 1989, the workers immediately decided to place Luke first on my list of art therapy "candidates." The workers told me they did not have much hope for this "problematic case" because of his hyperactivity, his hearing impairment, and the fact that he was "the only Indian child on the unit." The worker who brought Luke to the art therapy room for the first time sarcastically wished me good luck. After our first session, the counsellors and educators on the unit were in disbelief when I told them that Luke had responded well to art therapy, showing willingness and readiness to express himself through art. In my report, I concluded that he was definitely a good art therapy candidate. Soon after, the workers on the unit began referring to the art therapy room as "the place where magic happens once the door closes."

Luke's initial art therapy assessment revealed that he was able to express his thoughts and feelings, especially at the non-verbal level.

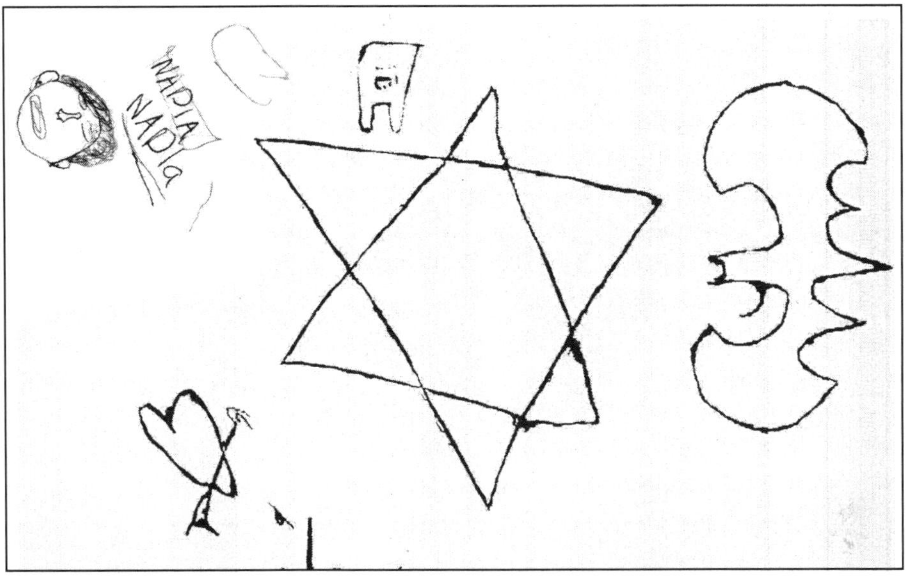

Figure 1.1s Luke's first picture

In his first drawing, he immediately drew a star, and then he added a heart, a portrait of me, a small boat, and a Batman symbol (figure 1.1).

Luke then described most of these symbols, which were repeated themes throughout his therapeutic process. He interacted readily with me and expressed his fear of the unknown, especially in terms of relating to his new surroundings (figure 1.2). Luke also mentioned how much he missed home, which was 750 miles away. When he painted figure 1.2, Luke was anxious about leaving to go back home to visit his family. He expressed his fear in leaving and he asked if I would still be there when he returned to the unit. He wrote my name in the centre of the heart, underlined it five times and then added the sun behind the heart with short yellow lines. The dark heart covering the bright sun, as Luke interpreted it, symbolized the tension and anxiety he felt within as well as the good things or sense of wholeness that were not yet known to Luke.

In our first sessions, Luke's open response to me was partly because he took me for a Cree person (because of my dark complexion and almond-shaped eyes). He derived much pride from his portrait of me, which he had included in his first drawing (figure 1.3).

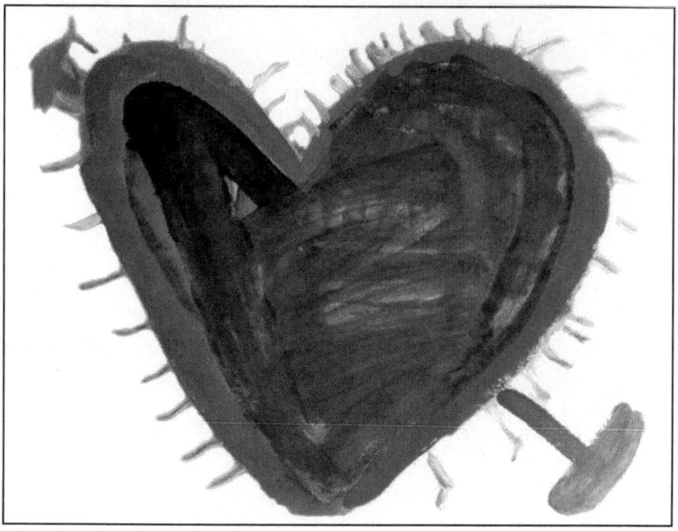

Figure 1.2 Luke's heart painting

Figure 1.3 Luke's portrait of me (detail from his first picture)

This boy engaged in two years of individual art therapy and, as a result, he developed a very significant relationship with me.[1] His successful treatment had a considerable ripple effect, leading to more referrals from various Cree communities in northern Quebec, as well as from Inuit, Ojibwa, Abenaki, and Mohawk peoples.

Luke's case illustrates two significant problems that I have faced during the past fifteen years of clinical work. The first is the Western approach to communication, which values verbal expression. The second, closely related to the first, is the preconceived notion that emotions must be expressed verbally in order to "properly" define an autonomous self. These Western-constructed biases create barriers when working with non-Western peoples such as First Nation peoples. I realized early on in my work that I was attempting to bridge ideologically constructed communication and emotional barriers within the context of art therapy. Art therapy is not free from the biases of the Western culture, which gave birth to the approach. However, what makes it distinct from classical psychotherapy is that art therapy is initially silent, because patients are encouraged to create a drawing, painting, or sculpture and, thus, to express himself/herself on a non-verbal level. Patients are then encouraged to talk about their iconic production; very often, they develop narratives about the imagery. It is possible that silence has a different meaning to the Crees, which I will further explore in this ethnography.

My experience in clinical art psychotherapy has shown that creating visual and sculptural media helps my Cree patients[2] transcend these emotional and political barriers in speech because it recontextualize emotivity and is initially a silent activity. In the art therapy context, the art acts as a catalyst for non-verbal emotional expression, which later facilitates verbal exchanges.[3] Although the language used – whether English, Cree, or French – also influences the actual verbal expression of emotion, I believe that for these Cree patients, the primary means for the expression of emotions is art, to which a narrative function is later attributed. In addition, unlike my Euro-Canadian patients, my Cree patients rarely hesitate when asked to draw in a clinical setting.[4] Most approach the art materials offered (e.g. pastels, paint, and clay) with confidence and demonstrate their readiness and willingness to engage in creating art even though they receive no formal training in childhood. They do not have difficulty seeing how the art-making process can be used as a tool in the resolution of conflicting feelings or issues, leading to the restoration of health. Many of my

Euro-Canadian patients initially do have difficulty understanding the link between art and therapy because art-making is seen as a special activity for talented individuals only (or is perhaps seen as childish). For many of my Euro-Canadian patients, art is marginalized in terms of self-expression, whereas it is not for my Cree patients. According to one of my Cree informants,[5] art-making is not perceived as an autonomous activity but as part of their way of life. One Cree woman, Lyne, explains: "It is important for us to see things visually. Even when we tell stories we say them with *words that are like pictures*. We are not writers, we are more visual. Art helps us see things and that's how we retain them."

It may be impossible for me to convey a definition of art for my Cree patients, simply because in the Cree language there is no word for "art." What I can judge, however, is the result: these individuals believe they feel better after engaging in art therapy. It may be that other factors are at work, such as the personality of the therapist or the environmental stimuli in which art therapy operates. It may be that the Crees who engage in art therapy volunteer because they want to be healed and so are healed, regardless of the therapy.[6] My Cree patients seem quite responsive to art therapy, as in the case of Luke. In this ethnography, I hope to explore why this is so, as well as analyse the elements of the art therapy space in which my Cree patients and myself continue to negotiate and engage. When I travel to northern Quebec Cree communities, I am usually provided with office space by local social services or the community hospital. I try to use the same office space whenever I return to the communities in order to maintain a sense of continuity. Sometimes interpreters are present during my sessions, usually with very young children (three to four years old) and elders who speak only their native tongue.

Many Cree people in the various communities in the Quebec north view art therapy as valuable and consistent with Cree forms of intervention. Art therapy is seen as a form of treatment that sets out to heal the spirit, mind, and body in order to restore balance in one's self-identity. According to my Cree informants, the healing process does not necessarily refer to mental health alone. It entails an approach in which one is healed when one experiences a sense of harmony and balance within the physical, emotional, mental, and spiritual realms. In addition, the individual is usually not isolated in his/her healing experience; close family members become directly involved in restoring the individual's health. Thus, my therapeutic stance in art therapy appears amenable to Cree discourses on healing, especially in terms of restoring balance in one's self-identity. This ethnography is not about Cree people as such but about individual experience with trauma, how it is perceived, defined, and narrated within the art therapy context, and how culture becomes an issue for my Cree patients in their healing process. Some traumas are possibly a result of their experience of political domination and cultural repression by Euro-Canadians.

I am aware that in the following study I am examining, representing, and, in a sense, defending Cree cultural conceptions that were given to me through images, words, and gestures by my individual patients and informants and that may not necessarily portray Cree society as a whole. I am thus representing a dimension of Cree reality, which, however, seems very important because it engages Cree definitions of the self, especially politically constructed definitions that reflect tensions and ambiguities in the Cree world that are very likely the result of colonial domination and repression. The focus will be on how the individual conceives himself/herself and how he/she articulates his/her world in terms of his/her social and cultural creations. Like Briggs and her experience of Inuit psychology and culture, I too have learned (and continue to learn) how Cree culture and psychology "actively reconstitute themselves and each other in the tangle of experience" (1998, 2). This ethnography is inscribed within the growing movement in anthropology that involves moving away from perceiving people as passive vehicles of their culture and social structures and toward approaching them as self-conscious and active individuals. I am also operating within a postmodern sensibility by including myself in this study, yet it is not essentially about me.

This book will help deconstruct the ideological dichotomy between Western notions of "self" and non-Western senses of "self" – in this case the Cree self – and perhaps show, as I have learned, that there may be more similarity than difference between the two and that the notion of self may not be that peculiar in the Cree context. Although there is not much published material on the Cree self, I have found similarities to it in studies on the Inuit self, especially in terms of how nature and the collectivity play significant roles in its construction. Moreover, these studies show how emphasis is placed on the individual's sense of autonomy, which also concords with the Cree self. Hallowell's classic 1955 ethnography on the Ojibwa, who are closely related to the Cree both linguistically and culturally, remains useful and fits well with my approach, especially his theory on the behavioural environment of the self. Among the Ojibwa, Hallowell noted that the self is perceived as an object existing in a world of objects other than the self, which is similar to the Crees' perception. In addition, I consider Hallowell's identification of animal images as expectable and non-pathological for the Ojibwa as pioneering, and it concords with what I have noticed among the Crees of Quebec.

Early on in my work, I came to notice a distinct difference in Cree notions of self from the definitions found in ethno-psychology and transcultural psychiatry, which tend to focus on non-Western notions of self as more collective-oriented. Thus, this study shows how the Cree self appears to be more of a composite-type self consisting of the individual and autonomous self, the self-in-nature, and the self-in-the-collectivity (these terms are defined in more detail below). Rather than viewing Cree notions of self as constituting an indigenous form of individualism, I illustrate how the Crees are highly individuated even though individualism is not a socially approved value.

I am also aware that my ethnographic description may distort Cree definitions and understandings by forcing them into my own ways of conceptualizing the world. The reality is that meaning can never be accurately translated and there are no simple elements of meaning (Rabinow and Sullivan 1979, 6), nor is "accuracy" the watchword it once was in the discipline. I plan to give voice from a variety of viewpoints from my Cree patients and informants in hopes of avoiding essentializing a notion of "Cree-ness" and painting a monolithic image of the Cree people I work with. Similar to Preston's 2002 ethnography, *Cree Narrative*, my goal in this study is to provide the reader with the subjective meanings of individual experience. Through their narratives and artwork, I show how the Cree individuals I work with articulate, formulate, and represent expressions of their notions of self, and, in turn, I develop an analysis of the images created by my patients and the verbal and non-verbal dialogue that emerges between them and me. My ethnography also highlights my own experiences and feelings in order to elucidate the relationship between what I know as a clinician-ethnographer and how I came to know it. I am aware that the construction of the Cree notion of self is in part constituted by my self-knowledge, and it is therefore important to provide the reader with my own experiences and feelings as well.[7] I hope to create a sense of the interplay of voices and actions, mine and those of the Cree individuals I have met and worked with, that results when distinct life experiences intersect and self-reflection and healing occur.

Since 1989, I have worked as an art therapist with approximately 1000 Cree individuals aged from three to ninety years old, mostly with the people of the James Bay region of northern Quebec. I began this research with the idea of exploring reasons for my Cree patients' response to art therapy. It gradually evolved into an analysis of how art therapy becomes a ritualized space where mythopoetic thought is evoked and where my patients and I transcend the immediate communication and emotional barriers between Cree and Euro-Canadian individuals. Often with my Cree patients, art therapy becomes a sacred ritual, in that it helps re-establish personal harmony through individuation. Through my analysis I developed a better understanding of the metonymic links my patients often make between art therapy and their experience in the bush, both constituting a place to re-affirm their notions of self. This research has taught me not only to consider the notions of self presented to me by my Cree patients and informants as a legitimate object of anthropological study, but also to observe my own relationships and feelings as significant data.

Chapter 2 outlines the ethnographic, cultural, and historical contexts of the Crees in Quebec. It is necessary to situate them ethnographically and historically because definitions of Cree culture are an issue for many of my patients in terms of the problems they face in identifying themselves vis à vis a culture at a collective and a personal level. Because the Cree collectivity – their identity as a group with shared traits, very much in the same sense of Anderson's "imagined communities"[8] – is constantly changing due to Canadian colonialism,[9] pressures and stresses are felt at an individual level as the elements with which individuals construct "Cree-ness" change in unforeseen ways. Cree styles of communication are explored in chapter 3, where I address the patterns of hierarchy and indirection in Cree conversation and emotional discourse and the Cree perception of human relationships as recounted in their narratives of self and their relationship with me. Barriers exist not because the Crees are "different" but because of the colonial ideology present in Euro-Canadian society. I show how we, my patients and I, transcend the communication and emotional barriers often present between Cree and Euro-Canadian individuals, especially in the context of mental health processes, and especially between individuals who invoke highly politicized definitions of "Cree" and "Canadian."

I am usually hired as a consultant for the northern health agencies, and therefore I am regarded as a figure with authority and expertise. The power relations in the therapeutic relationship between my "Aboriginal" patient and myself, the "white" therapist, are also imbued with socio-historical dimensions related to colonialism. Often with both my patients and myself, this remains an unquestioned reality. This ethnography addresses how this reality affects the emergent discursive practice in art therapy with my Cree patients.[10]

Chapter 4 examines specific elements of Cree mythopoetic thought such as narrative discourse and metonymic and metaphoric associations as exemplified in animal-doctor relationships. Synaesthetic elements of Cree reality are illustrated in one of my case studies. In art therapy, the Cree individuals I work with may be in the process of constructing a discourse that involves recreating myths in the context of their therapy with me. They appear comfortable with explicitly attributing emotions to their iconic production, which they say constitutes both spiritual elements and storytelling features[11] in terms of the emotionally filled narratives they express. Storytelling is a way of ordering and giving form and significance to the world, exemplifying mythopoetic thought by metaphorising it. The art therapy process appears to evoke the use of a mythopoetic reality set. "Mythopoesis … is a perception that arises when the content of thought is no longer the subjective means but the source of knowledge. The image recognized as "objective" is seen as belonging to the domain of meaning" (Meletinsky 1998, 93). From a mythopoetic perspective, the artwork can be seen as inheriting both the syncretic and concrete qualities of myth.[12] In both myth and art, the product cannot be separated from the process that produced it. The artwork and the narratives are seen as means to therapeutic ends.[13]

In chapter 5, I develop my argument of art therapy as a form of ritual activity: the physical space of art therapy (i.e. the structure and its limitations) becomes a place of meaning and what appears to be a metaphoric condensation of place and self, and many of my Cree patients make metonymic associations between their bush experience and art therapy ritual. Chapter 6, the conclusion, synthesizes the arguments of this study in hopes of elucidating the dynamics of how art therapy becomes a ritual space and an interstice for the expression of Cree self.

The art therapy that I am offering has been given a special status by Cree patients, Cree community workers, and other Crees who have been either directly or indirectly involved with art therapy. Near the beginning of my career, I met a male Cree elder who encouraged me to continue working with his people. His exact words were: "your art therapy was probably created for us to help us heal. *Aspaayimotam*. We have faith in you." According to this Cree elder, healing involves the restoration of "balance" that leads to a composed sense of self; this self relates to an individual's unique existence, and it is usually defined in relation to other people in the individual's environment. My own conception of self is similar to this definition because I view the self as having fluid boundaries that allow for other "selves" (i.e. significant others, including those personae that a person incorporates into his or her own social self) to play a role in continually redefining one's self. My own notions of the self as subject to being decomposed and healed and my patient-centred approach influence the formation of the art therapy context. I consider the "self" to relate to the distinct individual that we usually take ourselves to be.[14] Within the art therapy space I provide, it seems possible that their conceptions of self can emerge through the narratives. Preston's "ethnography of personal meanings" (2002, 68) similarly seeks the deep understanding of emotional dynamics through narratives, giving voice to the Cree narrators, and, as is here, the primary focus is on individually experienced and culturally patterned meanings. I also find relevance in Kerby's presentation of how narratives give meaning to the self, and how "the development of selves (and thereby the persons) in our narratives is one of the most characteristically human acts, acts that justifiably remain of central importance to both our personal and our communal existence" (1991, 1). Narratives also provide the patients with an opportunity to impose order on otherwise disconnected events and to create continuity between past, present, and imagined worlds (Ochs and Capps 1996, 19). Thus, in the following, I will attempt to show how my Cree patients contextualize their notions of self and illustrate how art therapy for the Crees has become a form of healing that is amenable to their conception of self as well as to mine.

2

The Crees in Quebec

In this chapter, I situate my subjects within various ethnographic, cultural, and historical contexts because images of Cree culture are an issue for many of my patients in terms of the problems they face in identifying with their culture at both a collective and personal level. The source of tension and instability usually lies in the representation of the collectivity used in (or forced onto) the composite Cree self. I present the materials that the Crees use to construct their ethnographic, cultural, and historical contexts, and I report what elements are available to the Crees who want to construct new identities, using elements they and others attribute to the past. Because I acknowledge that I can never know what they know, nor do I have the same social positioning strategies, comments in the form of personal anecdotes of our interactions will be presented as *ethnoprofiles*. These comments or statements made by my Cree patients and informants are indicative of Cree people's self-definitions. Also, my patients and informants felt that it was crucial for me to include myself in this ethnography, since, as they noted, I am the writer of this "story" and not them. This is consistent with Cree interactional principle, which in essence is dialogic.

THE ETHNOGRAPHIC AND CULTURAL CONTEXT OF THE CREES IN QUEBEC

In northern Quebec, there are nine communities and a total of 12,000 Cree inhabitants.[1] The Cree villages located inland count for nearly half of the entire Cree population in the province. The other villages are located along the coasts of James Bay and Hudson Bay. It is only within the past twenty years that the Crees began settling perma-

Figure 2.1 Cree home

nently in communities. The reasons for this previous resistance to sedenterization include the lack of employment in the settlements as well as the fact that the Crees preferred their traditional lifestyle and were experts at securing their livelihood from the land (Salisbury 1986; Niezen 1998; Atkinson and Magonet 1990). Although their economic self-sufficiency diminished once they began living in more highly structured communities, the persistence of culturally specific beliefs and ritual practices situated in a discursive space that incorporated many signifiers pointing to environmental referents has been quite strong. This is exemplified in the continuing importance of bush life for the East Main Crees of the James Bay region (Tanner 1979; Salisbury 1986; Preston 1981), in which traditional ceremonies are still held to mark the spring and fall hunts.

Ethnoprofile: I find this image (figure 2.1) is suggestive of the pressures of acculturation that many Crees are experiencing, in terms of settling within a house yet maintaining a wigwam in the "backyard." This home is about a decade old and this family, like many others, continue to cook in the wigwam in their backyard. When I once had supper at this family's house, they baked bannock bread in the conventional oven and cooked the caribou stew in the wigwam over a fire. It suggests the persistence of many Cree individuals I know who refuse to let go of ways of life they are familiar with and attached to. According to a Cree woman, who rarely cooks in the conventional oven "because it makes the food taste awful," the wigwam also symbolizes the sense of security the Crees experienced in the past, which she (like many) feels the need to hold onto, especially when so much has been destroyed or taken away. The experience of being in the wigwam (including the smell, the sounds, and the texture) while she cooks reminds her of her own childhood, and of a time when she felt safe and secure watching her mother and grandmother cook stew or smoke fish over the fire. "I knew one day I would be doing the same thing, so I had to watch them carefully."

In terms of Cree religious beliefs, Christianization of the James Bay Crees did not begin until the mid-nineteenth century, about 200 years after the establishment of the Hudson's Bay Company (Preston 1981; Salisbury 1986; Atkinson and Magonet 1990). According to many Cree elders I have spoken with, the importance of Cree religious beliefs was not acknowledged by missionaries.

Cree people did not become Christian because they were forced to. Many Cree people I have met believe that the teachings of Christianity are consistent with some Cree traditions. Cree beliefs already stressed the values of respect, sharing, love, and kinship (Niezen 1997), which the missionaries also preached. Thus, the Crees were not passive subjects of missionary persuasion. They showed their readiness and willingness to adopt the new ritual forms of values that they were already familiar with. Christianity was not considered incompatible with forest life and Cree religion (Niezen 1998). The missionary teachings may have been "reinterpreted to accommodate them to a Cree idiom of experience" (Preston 1988, 147). Preston claims that many Crees of the East Coast of James Bay manifested a form of syncretism, where they accommodated the spiritual elements of both religions. For instance, in the 1960s there were some Native Anglican catchecists who were also well-known traditional Cree shamans (1988, 151). Another example of syncretism was found in Cree narratives showing how traditional songs and symbols were combined with Christian hymns and icons. By the late 1960s, Pentecostalism began to spread, and, today, at least half of the Cree population are Pentecostal (Prince 1993). Prince notes that some Crees regard Pentecostalism as a necessary and positive force, since its severe rules of behaviour regarding drinking and sex have saved many from alcohol abuse and disruption in families. However, many Crees feel that its intolerance of traditional religious sentiments and expressions has had only negative effects on Cree culture and society.

According to the Cree elders I know, this syncretism or form of acceptance was not reciprocated by the missionaries, who preached against Cree social practices. Nevertheless, the Cree people were able to maintain their autonomy, especially in relation to their hunting technology, strategies, and rituals (Morantz 1978; Niezen 1997). Despite some pressures toward control and assimilation, many did not abandon their cultural heritage.

Another example of syncretism is the Cree form of medical pluralism, where Cree people continue to use local plant and animal products as their pharmacopoeia as well as modern medicine to treat health problems (Adelson 2000; Atkinson and Magonet 1990). Adelson stresses how the Crees constantly express their respect for animals and nature. The Cree term *miyupimaatisiiun*, or "being alive well," "connotes a set of meanings that are contingent on Cree beliefs and practices" (Adelson 2000, 61), such that values are inseparable from practices.

Essentially, *miyupimaatisiiun* relates to being able to hunt, engage in traditional activities, live well in the bush, eat the right foods, keep warm, and, especially, provide for oneself and others (Adelson 2000, 60–2). The Cree concept of well-being is definitely linked to their traditional foods and activities. Traditional medicine continues to be used informally with the Crees by the elders, who broadcast their knowledge and experience on the local radio, and by Cree administrators who try to include traditional practices in formal procedures (Niezen 1997, 486).[2]

Ethnoprofile: A Cree elder once gave me a tour of a bushcamp, showing me the different natural substances, such as berries and tree barks that could be burned and used for preventive medicine, protection from evil forces, and simply for luck and health. Some substances were used individually, while others were part of recipes to help soothe, treat, or prevent certain ailments. These recipes, according to this elder, were also used by their ancestors, and most people who live in the bush, whether permanently or intermittently, have knowledge of these natural forms of medicine and resort to them when necessary. He gave me a medicine bag with roots and sweetgrass and I was told to keep it with me to protect my spiritual health. Herbal teas are quite popular and they are used as medicinal teas. I was once given a tea to settle an upset stomach, and I was told it included hibiscus flowers, birch leaves, cranberries, and cinnamon bark. Another one used for colds contains juniper berries, spearmint leaves, red clover flowers, and other roots. Both were quite effective – in fact so effective, I continue to use these medicinal teas.

The bushcamp continues to play a significant role in the daily lives of the Crees. The bush, or *nuhchimiihch*, is regarded by many Cree adults and elders as a natural disciplinarian, with its own rules and rhythms to which individuals adapt, and Cree hunters have long noted that there is a beneficial effect on individuals who follow a traditional lifestyle (Niezen 1993). They look forward to their traditional ceremonies to mark the spring and fall hunts. They also go to the bush to gather their herbal remedies.

During the last two decades, there has been a gradual revitalization of Cree medicine and a return to sweat lodges, religious ceremonies, and the use of shamans. My Cree informants believe that the Cree people need to strive to maintain their customs and traditional ways because these are integral elements of their existence as an autonomous people. They also see the hunting economy as a mainstay of Cree society (Niezen 1993, 1998) on the symbolic level, even though the economics of the traditional lifestyle might mean individuals lose rather than earn money. In other words, people are willing to invest time and money to continue this way of life because the ties to the land this implies are considered vitally important signals of Cree desires to be autonomous.[3] By symbolic I mean that hunting is a way of life that is considered by many of my Cree informants as a significant sign of their cultural survival, as it links them to their cultural heritage. For many Cree people, it is fundamental that they see themselves as hunters, despite the fact that hunting represents approximately 40 percent of their economic returns (Niezen 1998). In both the inland and coastal communities I have noticed many signs of the perpetuation of a hunting way of life, such as people celebrating when a young, pre-adolescent boy kills a goose for his first time, and women working hard to build and maintain the wigwams and the bush cabins.

Ethnoprofile: Many of my initial trips to northern Quebec were organized by a non-Cree person, who was in charge of Cree social services for all nine Quebec Cree communities. Once, when I arrived in Nemaska

Figure 2.2 Goose break

there was no one around. The trailer homes, store, and Band Council offices were all empty – only dogs were roaming the snowbanks. Finally, a man arrived on his snowmobile and he informed me that everyone was in the bush celebrating goose break. Goose break is a seasonal goose-hunting ritual that usually occurs in the spring, and many Cree people go to their bush camps to hunt geese and gather with their families. This ritual sometimes occurs twice a year (i.e. spring and fall) in addition to moose break, which occurs in the fall, and both were totally unknown to me until this experience. The Cree man on the snowmobile thought it was so funny to see a southerner stranded in the village. He then (luckily!) invited me to the bush to stay with his family. After this experience I made certain that my future trips would be scheduled by Cree community workers. At another time, I was invited to attend a goose break ritual in the bush, where a young boy symbolically enters manhood with the mark of his first killing of a goose (figure 2.2). The goose head is hung in the centre of the wigwam, along with other animal skulls, for the duration of the festivity, which involves eating the goose, drumming, and dancing. The skulls, antlers, and bearskin, as seen in figure 2.2, are placed as tokens of respect to hunted animals.

Many believe that the Cree language is a significant aspect of their identity and is maintained by being in the bush, because mostly English and French are taught in the community schools. Crees see this linguistic instruction as a result of having been forced to attend boarding schools outside their communities for a period after the Second World War, where the Cree language was never taught or even acknowledged. According to one of my informants, people were often punished for speaking Cree. She would speak Cree to her friends because she feared losing her language. One day she was caught and the teacher actually cut a piece of her tongue. She said that this experience scarred her both physically and emotionally, but she said she promised herself to not let it destroy her spirit, and so every chance she got she continued to "secretly" speak to her friends in Cree.

My Cree informants see themselves as faced with a great challenge, involving problems such as alcohol abuse, violence, and suicide. These problems are seen as affecting their evolution and even survival as a people. Crees attribute these problems to the stresses of acculturation, which have developed from the "Whiteman invasion" and the subsequent social and cultural domination of the Crees. In order to cope with these problems, many Crees have tried to return to Cree medicine and treatments, sometimes used in combination with modern medicine. Some Cree people turn to the Christian Church and consider it a positive force in helping them deal with their problems. Among the Crees there appear to be demands for cultural pluralism, combining Christian teachings, Western biomedical practices, and Cree traditional approaches. This move toward cultural pluralism is suggestive of a dynamic and open Cree culture, but paradoxically may be inhibiting to individuals, who must seek and invent creative ways of reconciling these different and varied semantic and semiotic fields.

A QUEBEC CREE COMMUNITY

In this section, I describe a Quebec Cree community where many of my Cree informants and patients live. I provide empirical details of how they live as I have observed while working and living in this northern community. I use the pseudonym "Masgami" for this community in order to protect the identity of my patients and their families and friends.

This community was established in the early nineteenth century as an important fur-trading post. This post was also used for whale hunting. The first Anglican missionaries arrived in the mid-1800s and established a school in the early 1900s. Catholic missionaries began their activities in the 1920s, and they also founded a school and a hospital. Masgami was subject to a process of semi-forced settlement in the 1960s, when more than fifty permanent dwellings were constructed by the government as a means of facilitating government practices of the time, which favoured integration of Native lifestyles into a lower-middle-class model of Euro-Canadian values.

The present population of Masgami is approximately 2500, with 400 permanent Cree households and 200 non-Native people who work for the schools, hospitals, social services, and Hydro-Quebec. From a Euro-Canadian perspective, this community has all the "essential" services, such as running water, electricity, a local radio station, a police force, a fire station, and a general store. It is connected to other towns by a highway and several paved roads with clusters of houses. There are two churches, Anglican and Catholic. A commercial building in the centre of the community holds the general store, a bank, and a hair salon. A motel, the Band Council office, and other offices are on the second floor. Thus, there is a considerable amount of traffic in the commercial building. Adjacent is the community centre, which contains several offices, an auditorium, a restaurant, a reception hall, a gym, an arcade, and a bowling alley.

Some of the dwellings in the community are trailer-type homes, with two to three bedrooms, and others are larger homes with a cement foundation. These homes resemble a bungalow-style house with the bedrooms all on one floor. Although this community seems to resemble many other Euro-Canadian northern towns, there are several hints that the Cree residents have not modified their values just because some aspects of their physical surroundings evoke Euro-Canadian values. For example, I noticed in many homes that children do not necessarily have separate bedrooms. They often sleep with their parents, which according to several informants is a common practice. One person noted that it stems from being accustomed to sleeping all together in the tent. In many homes, I noted that a freezer filled with meat (goose, caribou, moose, and beaver) is usually found in the basement. On the outside, the homes are surrounded by 4x4 trucks, large vans, skidoos, and children's toys and bicycles. Although these objects are also owned by Euro-Canadians, Crees see them as useful imports that allow them to live their lives as they wish. The fact that they own and use Euro-Canadian goods does not mean they feel constrained to behave like Euro-Canadians.

It may be significant that animals in the community are also treated according to Cree beliefs. Dogs often roam freely in town. Dogs that are considered pets are usually owned by the Euro-Canadians who live in Masgami. Crees say that other dogs are owned by everyone; they are seen as "community dogs," as one informant told me. Like the children in the community, it is everyone's responsibility to feed them. Many of the Euro-Canadians in Masgami have great difficulty with the roaming dogs and feel the dogs are mistreated because they do not live indoors and are not leashed when outside. However, my Cree informant Sid said that Crees treat dogs with respect by giving them the freedom to roam. Sid related this to the past and how hard dogs would work in pulling sleds during hunting expeditions in the winter months.

Most revenues come from working for the Band Office, in social services, schools, and daycare centres, and for construction companies. Another important economic activity involves hunting, fishing, and trapping, and approximately 30 percent of the Cree population benefits from the Income Security Program, which provides a guaranteed income to hunters and their families who spend most of the year in the bush. Many Crees are determined to preserve income security for hunters because hunting is viewed locally as a profitable commitment for the community as a whole. Nevertheless, in Masgami the unemployment rate continues to be high, and many people receive welfare. This is often a source of tension for those Cree people who want to work but for whom the options are few. Many attribute their feelings of depression and inadequacy to unemployment, which often leads to alcohol abuse.

Several of my Cree informants believe that dependency on welfare and the Income Security Program has placed constraints on their bush activities. Many Cree people feel that the Income Security Program is contradictory because on the one hand, the government encourages bush activities, yet on the other, it provides a ceiling on the number of days in harvesting and related activities that are renumerated under the program. This contradiction between traditional freedom and Euro-Canadian control is often experienced as a source of tension. Many people have difficulty with the high transportation costs they have to pay for goods now seen as essential, such as Euro-

Canadian food and clothing. For instance, a pack of diapers costs $30 and a four-pack of toilet paper rolls $10. Often, Cree people stock up on such essential items when they travel down south to Val d'Or or Montreal. Although I have not been able to get the figures to calculate whether store profits are reasonable, some researchers (Lanoue 1991) have suggested that these stores in Native communities are continuing the tradition established by the Hudson's Bay Company in the fur trade period of making profits on individual trades to cover the risk of loss in the future. Although this might have been justifiable when transport was by canoe and boat, and Euro-Canadian merchants really faced losing their investment to accidents, this is hardly the case today. The high cost of living may also contribute to tensions among Cree individuals.

In addition, during the fur trade period, the Crees became firmly enmeshed in the mercantile capitalist economy, which favours an ideology in which individualism is accentuated. The notions of absolute property and contractual exchange were foreign to the Cree people (Dickason 1997), although individuality was not. However, stressing individuality is not the same as stressing individualism, which is often, for Euro-Canadians, another word for egocentric competition. Euro-Canadian economic practices, unfortunately, stress egocentrism characterized by competition and individualistic values, and these are reinforced by welfare and the Income Security Programs. Some of my Cree informants noted that these programs isolate individuals from one another and encourage dependency on Euro-Canadians rather than encourage a self-reliant community in which individuals cooperate with one another. One Cree man said that "the welfare and the Income Security Program are tools to enforce settlement life, imposed on us (the Crees) by the government." Undoubtedly, this is another source of great tension for many Cree individuals.

In terms of bush life in the past, local groups would go hunting within a given territory while respecting other people's hunting territories. The notion of territoriality was always vaguely defined, in the sense that these hunting territories were not seen as private property and did not have formal boundaries that prevented others from hunting. In general, people were free to move around and hunt where they thought best. In Cree society, stewardship and sharing are two long-standing principles of an individual's rights and obligations associated with the use of land (Niezen 1998, 16). The *uuchimaau*, or tallyman, is responsible for a designated hunting territory and including managing family activities within the territory, ensuring that the animals are not overharvested, and such obligations have remained unchanged to the present (Niezen 1998; Morantz 2002). The fur trade and, later, hydro-electric projects in northern Quebec led to the development of designated traplines registered with the government, and Crees were given areas to set up their bushcamps. Many Cree elders claim that before the registered trapline system, everything used to be in one piece and everyone respected each other's areas while sharing hunting territories. Before the trapline registration system, there existed a Cree tenure system with customary rules established by the Cree people. Nonetheless, it is by no means clear that the registration of traplines altered fundamentally the kin composition of multi-family groups on Cree hunting territitories, or reduced sharing and cooperation as regards access to territories. There was more of a continuity rather than a disruption in the territory/hunting group system because some aspects of the registered trapline system are consistent with Cree views on the freedom of individuals to act as they see fit.

Kin relationships were more than just links between genealogically or consanguineally defined individuals. Cree kinship values involved a system of social classification different than that of Western society.[4] The accent is placed on links among individuals as members of larger categories, though these are often not named explicitly as such, and so may be regarded as extended or fictive kinship. Turner and Wertman's model, based on the Shamattawa Crees of northern Manitoba, may be useful for understanding Quebec Cree social dynamics. According to Turner and Wertman (1977), Shamattawa Cree kinship terminology reflected an incorporative principle, in which ego-centred networks merged through the exchange of marriageable partners and local groups became allied. This model concords with Quebec Cree practices, where local groups are comprised of a conjugal pair (i.e. husband and wife and dependents), drawn from a larger unit that Turner and Wertman call brotherhoods.[5] Some fathers and sons hunted together, although surnames inherited through patrilines were not part of their social organization. This practice of collaboration between fathers and sons and sometimes between brothers gave early traders and anthropologists (especially if they never did any fieldwork among the Crees) the impression that the Crees were a patrilineal society, which is not the case. Unfortunately, this impression has lasted to this day.

According to Morantz (1983), the fur trade provided the James Bay people with more options in their subsistence patterns than were possible before. Morantz argues that subsistence was still the determining factor in terms of social organization, and so the fur trade could have generated a trend toward an expanding social organization. However, many of my Cree informants (mostly elders) believe the fur trade also forced people to move into new regions in search of new sources of furs for the trading companies and pressured them to value the individual benefits of individual accumulation at the expense of the needs of the group. Nevertheless, as mentioned above, although Cree values of sharing and sensitivity toward the needs of others (Tanner 1979) were not necessarily reinforced by the fur trade experience and may even have been subject to pressure, the fur trade did not fundamentally reduce the sharing and cooperation among Cree people. In fact, as Morantz (2002, 19) argues, archaeological findings show more of a continuity of Cree social structure than a dramatic change.

In terms of Cree kinship categories, "family" is not a stable category in the sense most Euro-Canadians and many anthropologists use the word. "Household" is a more relevant category, and it exists as a named grouping. There are no historical inclinations to categories such as "family," which was introduced by the missionaries and loosely adopted by the Crees, more in speech than in fact. According to one of my informants, in terms of family, *aa paayikutaausiich* is the term many Cree people use to refer to "a group of us." Other people's children, whether Cree or non-Cree, are always welcome in most of the households I have visited. I was once invited for supper at a Cree friend's house and I was surprised when five children walked in and immediately joined us at the table. The Cree woman noted that her house was their house and vice versa. This exemplifies the value Crees place on sharing as an effective means of countering tendencies toward individualism.

"Bands" continue to exist among the northern Quebec Crees and have evolved into administrative and political units, with officials that act as intermediaries between government officials and band members. There are thus three important social categories: the autonomous individual, networks (including "brotherhoods"), and the band. Some Cree people see these categories as traditional and as linking them to the past, and thus, when used, the categories become re-interpreted signs of the past in which Crees were not subject to Euro-Canadian bureaucratic and economic control.

Geographically distant relatives still retain strong ties within the community, and child-rearing is seen as a shared endeavour. For instance, as was described to me by Lyne, who is from Masgami, there is a ritual referred to as a walking-out ceremony, where a toddler walks out of a wigwam and onto the ground for the first time. Both Tanner (1979) and Adelson (2000) describe this rite of passage as symbolizing a child's entry into the world of the Cree people. According to Lyne, the wigwam is built in the bush specifically for the event and before sunrise of the day of the ceremony. The grandparents are usually within the wigwam and the parents await the child outside. Before this ritual, which usually occurs in the spring and at sunrise, the toddler should not be placed on the ground outside. Following the ritual, relatives and friends gather for a feast where bush food is offered (e.g. berries, caribou, and goose meat).

As for the Crees from Masgami and other Quebec Cree villages, they have always been experts at securing their livelihood from the land. Cree perception of the land as providing for human beings is sensitive to both spiritual and material concerns (Niezen 1998; Ghostkeeper 1996). Hunting is considered a "holy occupation" (Speck 1977, 72). According to my informants, "economic" actions are not motivated by profit, accumulation, and increase. There has always been a respect of land, animals, and for fellow hunters and their "families." The Cree way of life and religious beliefs and practices all revolve around complex beliefs regarding the relationship between man, nature, and animal. Hunting and religion are conceptually distinct categories of human practice, yet the animal plays a prominent role in both realms (Brightman 1993). Man is surrounded by forms replete with life like his own; thus, all beings and natural things, such as rocks, streams, and winds are thought to have a living soul.[6] All plants and animals have functional roles in the universe, which man needs to respect and use appropriately, whether for spiritual quests or medicinal or hunting purposes. In Cree cosmology, the natural world has restorative and curative powers (Niezen 1998). Although their economic self-sufficiency diminished once they began living in more highly structured communities, the persistence of traditional beliefs and ritual ceremonies remains strong. The bush economy continues to be a significant element in present-day Cree society and especially in definitions of the self, as seen in the village of Masgami.

THE HISTORICAL CONTEXT OF THE CREES IN QUEBEC

The Cree people of the James Bay area in Quebec have lived in the region for at least 5000 years (Salisbury 1986; Niezen 1998). Although the natives of James Bay Quebec have been known as "Cree" by the Europeans, Crees do not refer to themselves as Cree.[7] They call themselves either *iyiyuu* (coastal Cree dialect) or *iinuu* (inland Cree dialect). *Iyiyuu* or *iinuu* has four levels of meaning, depending on the context (Atkinson and Magonet 1990). On one level, it means "human," as opposed to other life-forms. Second, it relates to Native, as opposed to other ethnic groups. On the third level, it distinguishes the "Crees" from other Native nations. Finally, it means living or having life (Atkinson and Magonet 1990, 14).

Crees distinguish one another according to the areas they come from and by their hunting areas, the main distinctions being between the inland and the coastal people (Salisbury 1986). There were no permanent Cree communities before the European fur trade, and most Cree groups led a semi-nomadic lifestyle, with the entire "band" meeting and living as a group for only the brief summer months.[8] During the other three seasons the band divided into hunting groups that superficially resembled partnerships between extended families. Thus, the "band" or large grouping only functioned seasonally during the few weeks of the summer, usually assembling near a body of water with good fishing resources (Rogers 1963, 26). It did not form for political, religious, or economic reasons, although the most respected male member was given the title of "leader," and was often the shaman of the group (Rogers 1963; Morantz 1983). With intensive European contact and the subsequent fur trade, the features of the "band" and its functions changed as they assembled at trading posts, increased in size, and contained fewer shamans (Rogers 1963).

The type of "social organization" of the seventeenth-century large grouping or band was congruent with their hunting practices, since the northern Crees largely depended on animals, such as furbearers and moose, who have different territorial habits – the furbearers tend to live in confined spaces, while the larger ungulates on which the furbearers depend for food have larger range, yet are isolated and relatively scarse. Some groups also depended, to a certain extent, on animals like caribou, which necessitated a somewhat more complex but temporary hunt organization (Henriksen 1974; Riches 1982; Martin 1981).

According to a Cree elder I met in the bush, caribou meat and caribou hides used to clothe people, as well as birch bark used to build canoes, were valued trade items between the northern and southern Crees. As hunters and fishermen, the survival of the Crees through the years was based on their skill and intimate knowledge of the animals they hunted and of their environment. In fact, before the Europeans arrived in their area, the Crees were quite familiar with the fur trade system, carrying goods and furs from the St Lawrence northward to James Bay and south using canoe routes they developed (Morantz 2002; Francis and Morantz 1983).

In the mid-1600s, the English-European explorers found themselves among the largest group of Canadian Amerindians, whom they named "Cree." Civilizing the Cree people was not a priority on their agenda. Rather, establishing a positive relationship with the Crees was essential to the development of a functional fur trade system (Dickason 1997). The English apparently appreciated the hunting capabilities of the Cree hunters.

Both parties were willing to negotiate an alliance because without it trade would be insecure (Dickason 1997). The Crees, from their point of view, were negotiating a reciprocal relationship. They expected that the Europeans would help them when necessary, just as they would help the English. According to Dickason (1997, 117), unlike the English settlers, the concept of absolute property was foreign to the Crees.

Even though the Hudson's Bay Company (HBC) was established in 1670, many traditional aspects of Cree life were not directly threatened since a measure of co-dependency developed between the Company and the Crees: the Europeans depended on the Crees for food and furs, and they provided the Crees with guns and ammunition for hunting purposes (Preston 1981; Salisbury 1986), as well as for defence and war. In order to maintain this cooperative and co-dependent relationship, the HBC also kept out other Euro-Canadians until about 1870. The HBC often used Cree people as guides and hunters to extend its sphere of trade to the north as the Company's workers were inexperienced (Morantz 2002; Francis and Morantz 1983).

During the past twenty years, a new paradigm has surfaced in North American historiography, one that substitutes the old idea that the Crees were dominated from first contact with Europeans. With specific reference to the Eastern James Bay Crees, Francis and Morantz (1983) illustrate that for almost two centuries, beginning in the seventeenth century, the Crees had established a cooperative relationship with the English and French traders. In other words, it could be considered a business or strategic relationship (which of course is a more appropriate term from the Cree point of view), in which both sides obtained goods they each wanted without threatening the survival of the other. The Cree and the European traders, who were few, interacted along commercial, religious, and hunting frontiers. The Crees were valuable allies because of their ability to survive in the bush. At this point in the seventeenth century, there was no need to alter their ways because their hunting methods were successful and thus necessary for the maintenance of the trade system (Miller 1989). As Morantz emphatically sets forth, "during the fur trade period, the Crees still had the means and the power to define themselves. … The Crees seized opportunities and maximized their social and cultural options" (2002, 23). The Cree people were not powerless, passive victims, as depicted in many of the older accounts of Canadian history. They had an active role in the making of contact history.

Moreover, according to recent ethnohistoric research, Crees also played a significant role in the trade system itself and were crucial to all aspects of the fur trade until the nineteenth century (Morantz 2002; Francis and Morantz 1983). The scholars of this "enrichment thesis" view Cree traders as well as other Native traders as "rational and calculating in pursuit of their own self-interest" and not as "gullible savages" (Fisher 1992, xiii). In other words, during the eighteenth century, Native people as a whole were intelligent strategists and participants who were responsible for establishing the procedures of the fur trade. As one Cree elder explained, "My ancestors had had experience with trading before the Whiteman came. They would trade with other Indians all the time. The Whiteman needed us because they had no idea how to use the canoe and no idea how to hunt the animals. They showed no respect for the animals like we did, so we hunted." As Francis and Morantz also state, the Natives possessed the knowledge and skills to hunt and trap their fur-bearing prey, as well as for other animals that were part of their diet, thus making them necessary partners in the fur-trade enterprise (1983, 25).

From the late seventeenth century and their initial contact with Europeans, Crees manifested their pride and confidence in their cultural ways by not discarding their own technology and equipment in favour of European technology. They actually provided the European traders with essential tools, such as canoes, snowshoes, and sleds (Morantz 2002; Francis and Morantz 1983). Despite the close cooperation needed for the trade and the prosperity it brought to both sides, both the Europeans and Crees continued to live their separate and autonomous ways.

The nineteenth century brought profound changes to Cree-European relations. What was once an alliance became irrelevance as the Europeans began to view the Crees, as well as other Natives, as obstacles to economic development and as consumers – wasters – of public funds (Miller 1989). If they wanted to continue to participate in the fur trade economy, Cree people had to settle close to particular trading posts specifically during the summer months, which restricted their freedom of movement. They lost their roles of strategic allies and economic partners, and cooperation gave way to coercion (Miller 1989, 98). The Crees had to choose between traditional forms of redistribution of game and furs and a newer, individual trading partnership that some have suggested weakened group solidarity (Frenette 1985; Knight 1965; Leacock 1954). There were obviously pressures for the Crees to change and conform to Western market-oriented social and cultural models; for example, Crees who lived in the Hudson Bay lowlands area chose to monopolize access to European trade goods, acting as middlemen with other, more distant Native Indian groups (Morantz 2002; Francis and Morantz 1983). In brief, Crees often had to defend their territory from encroachment by outsiders, which sometimes forced them to use less-valued parts of the homeland in order to demonstrate their proprietary interest (Morantz 1980). Despite these pressures, the Hudson's Bay Company continued to limit contact with the larger European-based society, such that missionaries, governments, and corporations only slightly affected the Crees until after the Second World War.

Thus, although the fur trade brought change that the Crees could initially control, it also brought change in the long run for which the Crees were unprepared, which eventually culminated with their forced "integration" into the Euro-Canadian world in the period following World War II, including the implementation of boarding schools, the destruction of their political institutions, and the placement of Cree people in reserves. The Crees were often unable to cope with the new and disruptive elements that came with the forced conformity to Euro-Canadian bureaucratic procedures (Fisher 1992, 48). Cree culture and bush life were altered but not destroyed (Morantz 2002; Miller 1989; Francis and Morantz 1983).

Although the fur trade began the movement toward permanent settlement, its impact may not have been as profound as the combined influence of Anglican missionaries, formal medicine, and residential schools,[9] which all occurred at different times (Niezen 1998, 39). Missions, biomedicine, and schools, each in different ways, had a subtext of assimilation, integration, and domination with little regard for Cree values and ways of life (Niezen 1998). In fact, the fur trade had tried to keep Crees "intact" so they would pursue "traditional" hunting of fur animals. Missionaries, in contrast, had no such agenda.

The missionaries were responsible for developing the first hospitals and many residential schools. Cree religious values and beliefs were often considered by missionaries as "devil worship," and Cree healing practices were seen as primitive, fraudulent, and harmful (Waldram et al 1995, 98). Permanent communities were eventually built around missionary and government institutions and hospitals, which placed more pressure on the Crees to stay in the community, often for the sake of their children (Niezen 1998, 39). As a result, an opposition developed between bush life and community life. Residential education enforced European middle-class values and further distanced Cree children from their parents and relatives.

Ethnoprofile: A Cree woman with whom I spoke described her experience in a residential school as follows: "I was taken away from my mother's arms, put on a plane and I was promised to be taken care of. When I got there I was separated from my brothers and sisters and I was given a number, '37.' I lost my name, my family and when I was abused they took away a big piece of me. I was horse-whipped and placed in a dark room for a long time, maybe a whole week, with bread and water – just like a prisoner. I was told that I should never speak my Cree language again. After many years, when I returned home, I returned a different person but I never lost my roots. My mother was waiting for me."

Not all the Cree people I met had negative, traumatic experiences at residential school. Lyne, one of my Cree informants, said that she was not separated from her siblings and her experience at the boarding school was positive overall. She was "allowed" to speak her Cree tongue and she actually spent a lot of time with her siblings and friends from her own community. She did miss her parents and looked forward to returning home. Lyne especially missed her customs, the special rituals and gatherings in the bush, which she and her siblings engaged in as soon as they returned.

As with the initial stages of the fur trade economy, Crees were quite selective in their adoption of key features of European technology and medicine, ideology and religious culture. What Crees considered useful – tools and medical treatments – was adopted to supplement their own technology. Nursing stations with medical supplies were used for emergencies, and some Western medications were used to treat diseases such as influenza and scurvy, often in combination with a white cedar drink or a preventative diet of cranberries, gooseberries, and currants picked from the bush (Waldram et al 1995). In fact, the Hudson's Bay Company had made sure their "Indian" traders were vaccinated against smallpox in order to ensure the health of their partners, and the Native people often shared their medicinal pharmacopoeia with their European counterparts (Waldram et al 1995; Trigger 1985).

In terms of equipment adopted in the bush, several key manufactured items, such as snowmobiles and motorboats, as well as roads, have made transportation to the bush much easier in the last two or three decades. Hunting has been more successful with the use of modern rifles and shotguns, although it is doubtful Crees were eager to substitute "traditional" weapons with the earlier trade guns, which were often highly inaccurate and even dangerous to the shooter. Thus, when the Crees have been allowed choices, bush life has been more often enhanced rather than compromised (Niezen 1998, 7). Cree hunters have long used technology manufactured outside their own society with no feeling that their way of life was threatened, and their forest way of life has a long history of accommodation and innovation resulting from outside influence (Niezen 1998, 5, 7), just as there were extensive pre-contact trade networks. As Niezen (1998) notes, the use of rifles or outboard motors did not erode spiritual relationships with hunted animals because the Crees, like many other Native groups, did not use the new technology in a "Whiteman's" way; that is, they did not increase returns from the hunt but preferred to see the new technology as increasing leisure time and especially security. The adaptations of specific ideas and tools were selective and within established cultural patterns (Dickason 1997). In terms of their adoption of European medicines and elements of Christianity, it is important to note that a characteristic of Cree religion and beliefs is that a single cult or category does not have special access to spiritual power or healing abilities. Borrowing ideas and beliefs from other people has always been a common practice.

Ethnoprofile: During my first visit to the bushcamp, I realized how I romanticized the bush, thinking it is a traditional way of life untouched by Euro-Canadian influences because the bush is far away from the community. After many visits to different bushcamps and my interactions with people there, I observed, as Niezen notes, that there is a willingness to accept and initiate change within the limits of practicality (1998, 7). For example, while in the bush, I stayed in a cabin that was built with discarded building supplies left over from dam construction projects in the early 1990s.

The mega-hydro-electric project that was undertaken in the 1970s by the Quebec government was a pivotal change for the Cree inhabitants of the region (Salisbury 1986; Tanner 1999; Frideres 1998; Niezen 1998). The project was launched by the government without any prior consultation with the people who would be affected by it (Dickason 1997, 380). As Tanner notes, rapid changes, such as community relocation, were imposed without sensitivity to the local ways of life and without the participation of the community, which in turn induced a sense of powerlessness (1999, 124). Not only were large parts of their hunting territories flooded and the Crees forced to abandon some of their hunting and fishing activities (Tanner 1999; Richardson 1991; Salisbury 1986; Waldram 1988), the legal battle to preserve Cree land that ensued and which they ultimately lost forced them to explicitly repoliticize many aspects of "traditional" life, which up to this point was simply considered as "life." In addition, the development of vast reservoirs encroached on the migration patterns of moose, who as a result have shifted farther and farther north (Adelson 2000, 125n6; Coppinger and Ryan 1999).

The signing of the James Bay and Northern Quebec Agreement in November 1975 gave the Crees and Inuit limited regional autonomy, monetary compensation, and created forms of local self-government for each of the nine Cree communities.[10] This comprehensive land claim agreement removed the federal government's responsibility for much of Cree life and transferred it to Quebec and the Crees (Waldram et al 1995, 246), although local Cree control of their social life was limited. Although the Cree and Inuit people were given what appeared to be substantial control of their own political, economic, and social affairs, the final say remained with the provincial government (Dickason 1997, 382). This disempowerment under the guise of decentralization of powers is undoubtedly a source of stress for many

Crees, who often feel humiliated and frustrated by being given an opportunity for autonomy on paper that has never been fully realized.

The Crees negotiated a plan with the Quebec government for regional autonomy in education, health care, and the Income Security Program (Niezen 1998, 3; Feit 1985). The ensuing development and growth of Cree administration based on Euro-Canadian models did not necessarily mean that Cree values, goals, and strategies would be replaced by Euro-Canadian ones (Tanner 1999; Niezen 1998), though it was probably disturbing to many older people who had little experience in these matters. For example, many Cree people I have worked with at the Cree Board of Health feel that the board is a non-Cree organization and distant from Cree values in terms of its functions. Nevertheless, they are willing to try to integrate it as smoothly as possible into their society (Bearskin and Dumont 1991).

Ethnoprofile: The mega-hydro-electric project continues to affect the younger generation, as expressed in a drawing by a Cree adolescent boy who was very concerned about the negative effects of this project on Cree "traditional" life (figure 2.3). He added green to represent the bush and blue for water and then added a large red "X" over it. He noted: "This is what Hydro is trying to destroy, but they can't because the bush is part of who we are." Below the large "X" he drew trees, animals, and a cabin. He used most of the picture plane to show that bush lifeways will persist and survive. He felt empowered after completing this drawing. He was able to frame his anger and frustration and express a narrative. He was emphatic in expressing how disastrous this project has been for his people. He mentioned how his grandparents were not consulted as the government went about destroying their land and their home. "They were asked to sign some papers and then they were relocated from Fort George to a new site, renamed 'Chisasibi.' He added, "They were given money but nothing was going to replace their home. Where they lived was suddenly taken away. The whiteman tried to take the bush away from my people, but they can't – it is our way of life and will always be." (This drawing was completed in a testing milieu, where the boy was seen twice in the context of a research study on styles of emotional expression[11].)

At best, the Crees languished in benign neglect by government authorities and thus preserved some aspects of a lifestyle that were consonant with their traditions. At worst, the period after the Second World War led to massive government involvement in previously

Figure 2.3 Bush lifeways

marginal lands as economic development became a major Canadian political and social agenda. The result was loss of hunting territories and the imposition of White-dominated bureaucratic institutions that aimed at establishing national control over lands, a control that rarely, if ever, had Cree interests at heart. Thus, as Morantz (2002, 26) contends, it was not the fur trade that radically transformed Cree society but more the events of the twentieth century, especially when the government imposed powers and financial supremacy, creating an unequal economic relationship that eventually overwhelmed and disempowered the Crees. Nonetheless, the Cree people's ability to negotiate and adjust to subsequent repercussions testifies to their activism as well as their ability to accommodate to rapid social change with a sense of order and continuity (Niezen 1998, 11; Morantz 2002; Tanner 1999; Bearskin and Dumont 1991).

CREE IDENTITY ISSUES

In general, the problems of the Cree patients I have seen in art therapy often involve their struggle with their self-identity within their cultural identity as Natives living in Quebec. In other words, the source of tension usually lies in the component of the collective representation in the self. As a result of European colonialism, indigenous people were faced with cultural and existential crises, with effects still being felt after 300 years.

Ethnoprofile: During my cross-cultural research comparing different styles of emotional expression between Euro-Canadians and Cree people, I met a fifty-five-year-old Cree man, who was one of my Cree research subjects but not a patient. He gave me valuable insight into the continued struggle his people experience in regards to colonialism. From that point on, I realized how colonialism was not a thing of the past but that many individuals remain affected. He drew figure 2.4 to describe his current frustration. He made sure I was well aware that the particular test I was using was heavily culturally biased. This test is the SAT9 (Scored Archetypal Test with 9 elements), and it is a pictorial measure used to assess alexithymia (the inability to express one's feelings). For this test, he was asked to draw a picture using nine archetypes (water, fire, something cyclical, sword, character, refuge, animal, and a monster) and then provide a written narrative of his drawing. He made it quite clear to me that these archetypes stemmed from Western mythology and not Cree.

This man created the monster as symbolizing the European culture when it invaded Amerindian land and the decimation of Aboriginal culture began, which was seen as something cyclical or progressive. This Cree man scored quite low on this particular scale, yet he used the scale effectively to express his anger and frustration about the colonialism he and his people continue to face and struggle with.

Essentially, my patients appear to experience inner conflicts related to wanting to be something they are not anymore. In other words, as noted earlier, their notion of self is reciprocally embedded in the collectivity or the community, within which they seek a sense of belonging. However, the Cree collectivity, their identity as a group with shared traits, is constantly eroded by the negative effects of Canadian colonialism, such as the obligatory Euro-Canadian school system. The Cree collectivity is constantly changing due to Canadian colonialism. Pressures and stresses are therefore felt at an individual level as the referent "collectivity" adopts new and ambiguous meanings. The Cree collectivity is very similar to Anderson's "imagined communities," not only because traditionally the Crees had a more fluid concept of community compared to ideas in the Western tradition,

Figure 2.4 The Old Ways vs the New Ways

but because the newly emerging Cree ideas of community are never quite realized in practice. In relation to Cree people, their "imagined community" refers to their attempts to create a Cree collective cultural identity, relying on essentialized and reconstructed notions of history.

Individuals struggle to come to grips with a definition – "Cree" – that was not part of "tradition" and that is politicized in such a way that it has little resonance on the local and individual level. Cree indigenous or "traditional" definitions of what it means to be human are no longer fully functional. The school system bombards the Crees with images of self and of collectivity that are Euro-Canadian rather than Cree. Formal schooling opens up new options, yet many of these options are hard to operationalize because many Crees feel that the system forces them to polarize their lives.

The school system does not teach the Cree people how to function effectively in the Euro-Canadian world, and the values and orientations given to them are often rejected because they make no apparent sense to the Crees, or are not presented in a way that the Crees recognize as providing useful benefits. The curriculum includes English and French, and reading, math, and science are taught in these languages. Extracurricular activities include hockey, baseball, and film showings. According to the school officials, who are mostly non-Native, the curriculum is geared to facilitate the young Cree people's entry into the Euro-Canadian mainstream. Many Cree adults, who enter the work force and often go south to Montreal or Toronto, have told me how destabilized they feel and how the values they were taught in the school system did not address Cree values, such as the importance of oral tradition, elders' teachings, and bush lifeways. In essence, the elements of their composite self – especially the self-in-nature and the self-in-the-collectivity – are definitely missing in the curriculum. Also, many Crees believe that the high rate of suicide among Cree youth is strongly related to the destabilized sense of self.

Furthermore, "Cree" is no longer a universally valid (for Cree speakers) indication of a core set of values that helps situate individuals in social space. The mechanisms of integration to formally organize themselves as a collectivity have been challenged and eroded by Euro-Canadian policies. In addition, many Crees feel they cannot use indigenous definitions of self against Euro-Canadian definitions because Euro-Canadians cannot or do not care to understand them, and also perhaps they are too distant from new realities. This suggests their dilemma: "Cree" cannot be and is not a marker of an autonomous people (and of autonomous individuals), yet it is necessary (they feel) in all definitions of the self.[12] As Adelson also observed, the meaning behind "Cree" for the *iiyiyuu'ch* ("Cree people") derives from "the oral historical record and interpretations of the past as it is constituted through the retelling of stories of hunting and survival" (2001, 299).

People are reacting differently to new pressures and stresses, such as the growing presence of Euro-Canadians and their recent commercial exploitation of northern resources (e.g. the James Bay Hydroelectric Project). According to a Cree informant, his people used to be more in charge of their lives than they are now. He said: "[in the past] there were no outsiders telling us what to do, how to learn and when to hunt. It's different now. We're not in charge anymore." Many Cree individuals get caught in the paradox of two conflicting identities: the pre-contact Cree identity and the post-contact "Whiteman-Cree." In the latter, the category of "Cree" becomes a semiotically charged category of the self with political overtones. "Cree" is not only a culture of lifeways and values but has become a political category in opposition to the "White" or Euro-Canadian[13]. Francis and Morantz (1983, 12) note that as a result of modern political and social pressures, a consciousness of Cree nationality and ethnicity exists today that does not seem to have existed in the past, largely because Crees functioned effectively without these concepts. According to Tanner, it is only within the past decade that the Crees have fully developed a consciousness of being "Cree," especially following their opposition to the proposed Great Whale hydro-electric project in the 1990s (1999, 136). This political category is part of a larger category of aboriginality, which has become a politicized discursive field. As Adelson also notes, the Cree people "are not so much 'revisiting the past' as they are negotiating and constructing a new sense of themselves as Aboriginal Canadians" in a new, strange, and menacing political context (2001, 298).

Brass, a Plains Ojibwa who claims Saulteaux ancestry, defines aboriginality as a social construction that serves as "a 'dividing practice' [i.e. dividing aboriginals from non-aboriginals] produced originally by imperial ambition and used by colonial powers when confronting 'the others' whose territory they conquered" (1999, 18). The Cree people, along with other Aboriginal people in North America, are designated by special legal status based on historical relationships developed by the colonial encounters between Europeans and the Native populations (Brass 1999, 18), but they have now appropriated the oppressive term "Aboriginal" for their own ends, investing it with new meanings and semiotic referents, such as "The Aboriginal Healing Foundation" and "the Aboriginal Wellness Gathering," whose goals include supporting Aboriginal people in building and reinforcing community-based healing programs.

Alfred claims that most Native people live in a world of ideas imposed on them by others, which creates a form of internalized oppression (1999, 70), or what he calls a "colonial mentality." Colonial mentality, which has become part of the Native construction of self, relates to a mental state that blocks the viability of Native values and beliefs and assumes the values, goals, and perspectives of Euro-Canadian society (Alfred 1999, 70–1). Many of my Cree patients' issues reflect this concrete problem of internalized oppression by means of a negative and conflicted self-image. When the oppression is internalized, it results in self-hatred, and is manifested through suicide and death resulting from alcoholism (Duran and Duran 1995) and violence.

Those who are deeply affected by these pressures are usually seeking an imagined collectivity or an imaginary whole, and they sometimes are drawn to pan-Indian symbols and rhetoric. This nationalist movement arises from the discourse of an "imagined community," which relies on essentialized and reconstructed notions of history, and it appears as an illusory inclusiveness (Boyarin 1994; Anderson 1991; Fernandez 1986). Nonetheless, as Shkilnyk (1985) claims, it is difficult to assess to what extent the past is idealized, yet the nostalgia that is strongly expressed is an indication of people's ambiguous relationship to the past: the "past" they recover in constructing politicized social identities may not be congruent with other "pasts" tied to the politics of individual memories.

Pan-Indianism is founded on a romanticized notion of aboriginality, linked to a former way of life that has disappeared, if it ever existed at all; it includes various images, ideas, and themes, such as that all Aboriginals possess a special spiritual wisdom connected to nature and the environment, often referred to as Native spirituality. Pan-Indianism is characterized by an idyllic interpretation of a past where unity reigned in the absence of conflict (Lanoue 1992).[14] It posits a brotherhood of all Native people, a universalist position as such where particularities are not considered. It is a nationalist rhetoric and a representation of a collectivity within which the individual remains subsumed. This collectivity has very few local manifestations, if any. The pan-Indianism movement is directly related to the discourse on aboriginality, which is largely promoted by the dominant non-Native society, which tends to romanticize aboriginal people and clump them together in one group rather than recognize the inherent cultural diversity within the "group."

Pan-Indianism informs and shapes the political rhetoric of the Crees that is sometimes manifested in the Cree Band Council and the Quebec Assembly of First Nations in order to promote the Cree people as a nation. This has had some positive results, especially in terms of the Crees' struggle against government plans to create more dams and flood more Cree land (Niezen 1998, 8). However, many of my older Cree informants believe that this movement, along with new "Cree" political organizations, represents White and not Cree ideology. A sixty-five-year-old man told me in an emphatic and angry tone that those involved in such groups are "government puppets talking the Whiteman talk, not Cree." The proponents of the "Cree movement," as among the Sekani in British Columbia described by Lanoue (1992), are usually from the younger generations. They believe that they need to form a Cree Nation in order to build a stronger resistance against large-scale development and to accommodate to rapid social change (Niezen 1998, 11), and that this "Nation" must in some ways conform to a Euro-Canadian model if it is to be effective as a symbolic agent for resistance and revitalization. From their perspective, regional administrative autonomy is not seen as a threat to the distinct lifestyle of Cree people. What many of my informants agree upon, both young and old, is that Cree cultural ways, hunting, trapping, and ceremonial events, remain persistent elements that are alive and well today.

Cultural constructions do play into the social and political dimensions of social control and disempowerment. How the individual is engaged in all of this is important. As Niezen claims (1998, 11), it is misleading to focus on domination and social pathology without considering individual response to social crisis. The issue is not only the imposition of social rules by Euro-Canadians on Crees – a political phenomenon, in other words – but also how an individual reacts psychologically to the mixed and sometimes contradictory rhetorical grab-bag of symbols at his or her disposal, and how tradition defines the terms of access to this cultural mix of symbols. In terms of individual responses to this cultural phenomenon, some seem unable to negotiate this access, while others seem to master the ambiguities in a way that is personally meaningful because their vision is socially accepted. Not all Crees feel oppressed. Sometimes Cree individuals are not "sick," but they know the language of the oppressed and are simply scared of the choices they must make. In this sense, many Cree individuals manifest a state of learned helplessness. Many are not taking responsibility because they never had to in the ways they must do so now – traditionally, people had limited choices in defining themselves vis-à-vis the collectivity, and these choices were essentially coherent with one other. Several of my informants have told me they feel that they are part of the immediate cause, yet the ultimate cause remains the Whiteman. Thus, the cultural phenomenon or acculturative stress is different from the psychological phenomenon. Cree people, although they prize individuality and personal autonomy, have coherent rules that define the manner in which culturally accepted expressions of stress are individualized. In other words, stress is culturally rooted, not physiologically controlled. For example, when a Cree individual gets stressed, he/she will often direct the violence and tension inward rather than toward others.

Along with traditional beliefs, Cree elders have standard sociopsychological guidelines or coherent rules for the young; however, it is common practice to not impose them on the young because they need to discover the "rules" on their own. This appears to create a paradox that has caused psychological stress particularly with some of my younger Cree patients, who meet with disapproval when their behaviour does not conform to the elders' expectations but receive little practical guidance on how to integrate the mixed symbols defining Cree selfhood. The extent to which traditional beliefs exist among the young varies, where some are familiar with them while others are not because they have little contact with their elders.

I believe that the way stress is experienced is directly linked to notions of self. According to Bob, my Cree informant, "the Cree self is always connected to something else. It doesn't exist alone. Each person is like a grain of sand existing among others." This definition alludes to the composite Cree self, where in each individual self there is a social and natural component. What Sampson describes as an ensembled individualism, a form of sociocentrism, concords with this Cree conception of self in that it is based on a more inclusive notion of self, where others are included in the region defined as self (1988, 16). In other words, in this form of sociocentrism, the sense of self is defined through the relationship and connection with others.[15] Stairs' definition of ecocentrism, with "eco-" encompassing human, animal, and the environment, is also relevant to the Cree notion of the composite self. The "ecocentric metaphor" is described as "an active process rather than an entity image, and one that includes the full environment directly, rather than only via the body of human society" (1992, 120). In this form of sociocentrism, the region defined as self includes others as well as animals and plants on which people depend and features of the landscape in which people live and move. This type of psychology allows for multiple definitions of the self, yet each is autonomous and on an equal footing with other social selves. In Western society, what is dominant is an egocentric mentality, a self-contained individualism in which the self is perceived as existing among others yet the self/other boundary remains firm. Each self is an entity separate from every other entity and from the whole group, and the emphasis is placed on self-authorship and personal control (Sampson 1988).

Stress in Western society is often manifested differently than in Cree society. Social and political problems cause stress at the individual level more so than in the social dimension, since Western individualism is an explicit and ontologically legitimate category into which various and complex meanings can be injected. Essentially, ideological purification of available identity symbols means that the cultural mix of available symbols and rhetoric is less rich and varied than among Crees, who privilege dreams as the means of establishing the ontological legitimacy of the individual. These dreams often involve contact with a variety of animal-doctors, and so some aspects of the self are very complex indeed. Like the Crees, among the Ojibwa, dream experience is interpreted as an actual experience of the self that in essence functions to maintain the sociocultural system (Hallowell 1966, 271). There is a huge gulf for the Crees between personal autonomy (individuality), which is highly valued, and individualism in the form of egocentrism, which is not. In other words, Crees are highly individualized as they value personal autonomy and recognize individuality but individualism is not a socially-approved value. Preston also makes note of the Cree value on individual freedom, which fosters creativity in the expression of individual style. However, as he points out, it is important to recognize that "individual freedom in Cree culture is regularly mediated by a strong sense of social practicality" (2002, 74).

In the West, people seem to have much greater freedom in the way in which they construct social identities, yet there is a presence of an ideologically legitimate individualism that is entirely absent in Cree society. In part, the strength of ideology explains the apparent paradox between ideologically legitimate individualism and the widespread conformity that is typically of Western modernity and, now, post-modernity. Ideology does not "control" thought as such but imposes limits on the thinkable so as to reinforce institutional spaces. In turn, institutions, especially political institutions, directly control an individual's movements, thus urging conformity at the level of thought. In brief, stress in Western societies is conceived as a tension between the individual and society, and coping with it is an individual problem. The onus is placed on the individual to deal with his/her daily stresses and anxieties. The difference I noted with my Cree patients is that the responsibility to address an individual's problems is shared among the individual, his/her family members, and Cree community workers, each playing a significant role in the individual's well-being.

In Cree society, while there may appear to be fewer stressors as such on the level of daily life (e.g. lack of competition), there is more stress in the ontological dimension of identity legitimacy because of the multiplicity of signs of the new collectivity (as I described above) and because of the weight individuals give others when defining the self. Integrating the composite self was already stressful, given contact with animal-doctors and the necessity to include the group in some form in the self. Problems such as substance abuse and suicide have become serious in Cree society, and Western medicine treats these as individual problems when in fact they involve not only the individual self but also the self-in-the-collectivity. Thus, the tragedy of these problems is also social in nature and consequently, there is a world of difference in cause and meaning to substance abuse and suicide. Furthermore, these problems have developed into a well-defined sub-culture that is learned by the young as an alternative or even a primary means of identity construction. As a result, many children and adolescents have grown into dysfunctional adults who possess a negative self-image.

In terms of their identity issues, the paradox many are experiencing is that they want to be something they are not anymore. They believe there is no stable Cree identity because of the continuation of colonialism. These individuals are engaged in an ideological positioning of placing one collectivity and way of thinking against another. They feel they need to adopt one over the other; they believe they will lose their cultural heritage if they adopt Euro-Canadian values and, on the other hand, they feel that if they re-invest in their cultural heritage, they will not be able to be effective in dealing with the Euro-Canadian mainstream. This struggle directly affects their self-identity by causing insecurities and uncertainties. The goal in therapy is to find a comfortable medium to help develop a more secure self so they can more easily integrate ambiguous identity symbols.

Many Cree people I know are fully functional in both Euro-Canadian and Cree contexts and they are attempting to resolve this tug-of-war crisis by engaging in a "cultural brokerage" (Stairs 1992) or "dual lifestyle" (Niezen 1998), deriving aspects of Euro-Canadian ideology and applying them to their Cree cultural base.[16] My Cree informants who are not experiencing this identity struggle are able to use their traditional knowledge, engage in rituals, and relate to Cree cosmology, and they continue to accommodate to the Euro-Canadian culture without disconnecting from their Cree cultural base. They are able to maintain and cultivate their cultural identity while acculturating to Euro-Canadian society. Many of my informants believe that their identity emanates from the past and accommodates to the present.

The Cree way of life has "a long history of accommodation and innovation resulting from outside influence" (Niezen 1998, 7). My informants often relate to how their ancestors found essential congruences between old beliefs and missionary ideals. Problems like conflicting identities arise "when you let go of spiritual relationships and replace it with Christianity alone because you lack the foundation that is Cree," according to a Cree elder.

Nevertheless, for many individuals the transition from tradition to modernity did not lead to a form of dual lifestyle or cultural brokerage. Instead, two incompatible forms of life met head-on in all Native communities and led to conflict (Ryan 1992). One of my Cree informants, Mary, eloquently describes this struggle in her own terms: "Culturally, I feel more like a Euro-Canadian person than a Cree person when I am around Crees. Most of my cousins are half White and half Cree but they feel Cree because they grew up in the north. Being Cree to me, you must have experienced the life of living in the community and know the language and the people. Also, being Cree is knowing the traditional life and not thinking of it as mystical, it is just the way it is." Mary is describing how things are grounded in experiential reality for many Cree people, and she is also expressing how her sense of self is destabilized because her "newer" Euro-Canadian identity is not grounded in a set of well-defined practices.

In Euro-Canadian society, emotion, symbols, and thought processes are heavily affected by ideology. Ideology is a centralizing and totalizing modern value field because it shapes our perceptions of ourselves as autonomous selves vis-à-vis other autonomous selves. Euro-Canadian ideology resembles Victor Turner's 1969 concept of ideological communitas, which consists of formulated views on how people should live that underline optimal social conditions. Euro-Canadians live up to a purified, ideal social identity of the self that is embedded in individualism in the form of egocentrism, in which the self is the centre of all things.

Foucault's concept of "technologies" in relation to power and self is relevant to my argument here, especially his description of technologies of domination and self (Martin et al 1988, 18). According to Foucault, what he calls "technologies of power" are essentially instruments of social control, which are recognized means by which groups control each other. Technologies of power determine the conduct of individuals, and technologies of self relate to how individuals are influenced to transform their bodies, souls, thoughts, conduct, and way of being in order to attain a certain state of happiness, purity, or wisdom. According to Foucault, these specific technologies imply certain modes of training and modification of individuals, and they are associated with domination. One's own behaviour is evaluated by the codes of the ideal self and role behaviour is articulated to meet the demands of interpersonal situations. Lotman (1990, 35) describes Western culture as less dynamic than most non-Western cultures because it enforces an ideology that promotes social passivity by encouraging the tendency to acquire truth in the form of prepackaged information. Thus, ideology is a centralizing form of discourse that focuses on a single modality of experience, which in turn leads to an individualistic definition of self.

Crees, on the other hand, do not have ideologies as such. What they have are values and belief systems that allow for multiple starting points for processes that define the self (because they are based on mythopoesis) and are far from constrictive (because on another level, they underline autonomy).[17] Belief systems are not necessarily ideologies. However, a society's widely held beliefs are not necessarily made coherent by ideology, and in societies without ideologies as such, beliefs can be easily linked to mythopoetic thought (Lanoue 1998). Lotman (1990, 35) would describe Cree culture as more mobile, dynamic, and more oriented to messages derived from a large number of cultural "texts" (such as myths) that promote knowledge. Ideology entails a centralizing and totalizing discourse of the self, whereas a mythological system allows multiple interpretations within a single discursive style (Lanoue 1995). The emphasis is placed on individualized perceptions and individual experiential meanings rather than on authoritarian, controlling definitions (Tanner 2000). The Cree individual is conceptualized as actively involved in the environment, and the self is located in a set of actions that are not necessarily meant to be congruent with one another. Individuals engage intimately with one another and, moreover, with non-human beings. There is no dualism between nature and humanity, and personhood is not restricted to human beings. Rather, the human is one of many forms of personhood (Ingold 1996). As we will see in chapter 4, animals play a significant role in helping individuals construct their identity. In chapter 3, we see how my Cree patients and informants communicate in the clinical context as well as in the bush and in the community.

3

Cree Styles of Communication

CREE INTERACTION PATTERNS

Studies in the area of ethnography of speaking have focused primarily on the analysis of verbal repertoires, defining discourse as including all forms of verbal communication (Finnegan 1992). Discourse is more than mere talk to create sentences and it can include oral forms, written texts, and kinesics.[1] This focus of discourse analysis, being largely concerned with verbal communicative acts, has consequently distorted the realities of communication in societies where non-verbal repertoires are common, such as Amerindian societies.[2] Sherzer exemplifies this point of view: "Discourse is an elusive area, an imprecise and constantly emerging and emergent interface between language and culture, created by actual instances of language in use and best defined specifically in terms of such instances" (1987, 296). A specific area that is analysed here is the narrative discourse of the Cree people, which is used as a communicative style within the therapeutic context. I am concerned with how people do things when they are speaking, writing, and creating artwork. In this definition of discourse, we see the interplay between speech acts and image acts. As Darnell argues, "the Cree case suggests that consideration of the speech-centered model of interaction is due for some modification" (1988, 77).

When I first began working with the Crees, I was not used to their typical sarcasm, resigned laughter, and indirect responses to direct questioning. I was also totally unfamiliar with their use of silence, which is often used to convey specific messages.

One time, two Cree women picked me up at the local airport in northern Quebec. In the van, sitting beside me, was a dead beaver, his eyes staring into mine for the whole two-hour trip to the village. The women made sarcastic remarks in Cree and then translated them into English and they giggled at this "southerner's" difficulty with being so close to a dead animal. Once I accepted the beaver and their sarcasm and laughter, simply because I did not have much choice, a silence set in for the next hour. Interestingly, the message conveyed in my silence was one of acceptance of their culture-specific ways of doing things, and I soon understood their need to test me, being a "whiteman." I came to understand that silence is not considered a void in communication among the Crees, in contrast to how we Westerners see it. Similar to what Brody describes in his work on Athapaskan hunters, I too discovered that "an awkward pause is a very rare thing among people who accept that there is no need to escape from silence, no need to use words as a way to avoid one another, no need to obscure the real" (1981, 44). My understanding of the Cree people's interaction patterns began to develop due to encounters such as this one, and as I became more sensitive to their thoughts and to the other registers of communication that they use, my initial, superficial perception of the "stoic Indian" faded quickly.

In Basso's 1970 study of the Western Apache's interactive patterns, he found that the Apache's decision to speak or be silent depends on the nature of their relationship to the other person or people, and the Cree people I know are quite similar in this regard. In contrast, silence among Euro-Canadians is often cued by the social setting (for example, in funeral homes, etc.) and not by the relationships within a setting. For example, when someone is sad it is courteous and considerate not to attempt to engage him/her in conversation. In addition, direct questions designed to elicit specific responses are usually interpreted as an attempt to control another person's behaviour. In fact, I have noticed that it is important to wait until people are ready to engage in a conversation before asking questions. This interactional strategy is the expression of how Cree people value non-interference and respect individual autonomy, which in turn helps promote functional interpersonal relations by discouraging coercion, whether it be physical, verbal, or psychological (Brant 1990, 535). As I was also told (or warned) by one of my informants, coercion or an attempt to persuade another person is often considered undesirable behaviour, and almost any direct question that requires an answer is considered coercion. For example, "how old are you?" is an innocuous question to us, but not to the Crees.

Cree people have sometimes been described as taciturn and reserved, and there is a tendency by Euro-Canadians to relate the absence of verbal expression with the absence of feeling. However, as with many other Native Americans whom I have worked with, the major function of speech is instrumental rather than expressive (Darnell 1988),[3] because there are other modes of expression that are as important as speech. The amount of talk is a relatively minor feature of Cree communication. Reticence among the Crees may be a form of control over excessive self-expression (Preston 1976), thus showing how the regulation of talk is aimed at limiting personal exposure and preserving intact a person's autonomy. Preston claims that by Eastern Cree standards, "we [Euro-Canadians] mask our true feelings with a conspicuous flim-flam of over-expression; that we sometimes even confuse ourselves, as to what the real feelings are" (452). Most of my Cree informants believe that talking excessively leads to superficial expressions of one's personality. According to them, a more limited self-expression fosters sensitivity and an in-depth understanding of interpersonal relationships. As one Cree elder informed me, there is no value in verbal communication if there is no asymmetry of knowledge between the speaker and the listener.

HIERARCHY AND INDIRECTION IN CREE CONVERSATION

As in all societies, there are implicit hierarchies involved in the regulation of talk in Cree society. However, hierarchy figures in conversation among Cree people in a different way than with non-Natives. In Cree discourse, hierarchy is implicit and the dimension of responsibility plays a significant role. Hierarchies and their semiotic "charge" are individualized and silent rather than socially acknowledged, and they are not sanctioned by ideology, as they are in Euro-Canadian rhetoric.

In the therapeutic context with my Cree patients, speech acts[4] such as maintaining eye contact and expecting an immediate response are avoided because they are seen as authoritative and thus invoke the threat of concretizing implicit hierarchies. In brief, Native American societies tend to avoid evoking and establishing the authority of discourse, particularly if the discourse serves as the basis for a judgment or a course of action having serious social or personal consequences (Hill and Irvine 1992, 6) that would explicitly confirm a person's power over another.

Cree discourse appears to downplay intention, yet the speakers remain responsible for their messages. The dimension of responsibility is concerned with the act of speaking itself; there is an allocation of responsibility for taking on the participant role of speaker or listener (Irvine 1992; Shuman 1992; Rosaldo 1982). Attributing explicit responsibility to the social situation would tend to grant discursive legitimacy to implicit hierarchies and is thus avoided. Irvine's analysis of the implicit hierarchy found in Wolof conversation is also relevant to the Cree people I have worked with. She states that "notions of personal responsibility, whether in talk or in any other activity … are not absent, but they are qualified by the hierarchical framework" (1992, 112). Formal speech, indirection, and delayed responses to direct questions are three important mechanisms in Cree society, as in many Native American societies, for establishing communicative responsibility while avoiding the formal legitimation of authority.

Irvine illustrates formal political speech events among the Wolof, Mursi, and Ilongot natives. She describes the structure of speech events and shows how there is more of a centralized focus of attention where only one person speaks at a time, as, for example, with the Ilongot. Also, different positional identities (social and personal identities) are invoked by the structuring of discourse (Irvine 1979). Formal, highly structured speech creates an imaginary space in which speaker and listener can disengage from the consequences of the messages (Lanoue 1991). This space is very much akin to mythopoesis, where myth is contextualized in the form of discourse, which will be discussed in the next chapter. These properties of formal speech are especially relevant to the Crees within the art therapy setting.

For example, I was giving an art therapy workshop to Cree community workers, and after presenting a case study, I attempted to open a discussion with a question regarding the case. Fifteen minutes passed until someone stood up and said, "You look frustrated because we didn't answer right away. We like to take time to think before we speak, especially about something this important." After this eye-opening experience, I began to gain a better understanding of as well as patience with an interaction pattern that was outside of my own comfort zone, but one I needed to adapt to in order to continue working with Cree people.

A related feature of Cree discourse is indirection, wherein speech rarely conveys explicitly what the speaker means at the level of semantic content. Cree indirect discourse reconciles both personal intentions and societal coherency. According to Farkas (1986), the proper etiquette for many Cree people is to present deflective responses to questions, that is, responses that are indirect so that an answer is not directly given in response to a question. This communicative pattern reflects a desire to not expose the self and offend the other, and it is directly related to the ethic of non-interference (Brant 1990).

Unlike the Fiji and Afro-Americans described by Brenneis (1987), Cree "talk" does not appear to have been transformed by colonialism because indirect discourse has always been an ongoing individual and cultural practice. Indirection can also be engaged literally, as when Cree speakers answer a question directly but address their speech to a third party and not to the asker.[5] Western therapy, with its emphasis on dyadic patient-therapist relationships, may be ineffective in this context.

All cultural aspects of Cree social life are geared to making sure that the structurally produced tension between group and individual interests never erupts explicitly. This implicit individuality, which does not at all resemble the explicit emphasis on individuals in Euro-Canadian rhetoric, has as its result a discourse in which common interests are rarely explicitly engaged. The result is very often silence, a silence that may not favour the development of new strategies of political survival in the modern world because it is geared to managing conflict among autonomous selves, not managing potential conflict between self and the group. In contrast, Western codes of healing implicitly legitimize explicit hierarchies and a rhetoric of alienated individualism, where the doctor-therapist as the authority figure is ranked above the patient, who is seen as helpless; these codes are thus inadequate in dealing with most Cree problems. In Cree healing practices, such as those administered by Cree shamans or healers, there is a strong individualistic flavour. However, in the process, the individual is not isolated, as family members and the community play a crucial role in the treatment of the individual, just as they do in the definition of the self among functional individuals.

EMOTIONAL DISCOURSE

"Emotions" in this context does not mean the full range of the biological traits of emotion (Ekman 1984; Izard 1977). Nor is the old Cartesian debate of the relative weight of nature or culture on emotions the issue. Briefly, the nature-nurture debate is a false dichotomy because it does not take into account how biology and culture work together in the process of identity formation (Erchak 1992; Hinton 1993). My Cree informants seem to believe that emotions are both cultural constructs and products of biology. In other words, emotions are seen as languages of the self (Lutz and White 1986) that are influenced and shaped by culture and society, and they are also bodily expressions (Scheper-Hughes and Lock 1987; Douglas 1970; Blacking 1977).[6] According to my Cree informants, feelings are experienced and expressed in the body, that is, they relate to the feeling by saying it is in the heart, head, or stomach, for instance. What may be elusive as a Western notion becomes a tangible one for my Cree informants because it is thought of as embodied.

For example, the Cree word that comes closest to the English term "emotion" is *umituunaaichikanich*, which is defined as "mind and heart, thought and feeling" (Scott 1996, 73). This definition is quite similar to Rosaldo's (1984) findings on the Ilongot and to Wikan's (1990, 1991) findings on the Balinese, where emotions are better understood as "embodied thoughts." Emotions are best seen as interpretations of experience in which the body and the self are immediately involved (Rosaldo 1984, 141). Emotions *are* important to the Cree individuals I have met. However, the verbal expression of emotion may not have been developed because it may not be valued when interacting with humans. What we call taciturn and emotionally reticent may not be applicable to the Crees since they recognize few occasions in which it is obligatory to express their emotions. Now that they are being educated in the Western sense, many Cree people are learning that one aspect of the Western identity kit is the ability to express verbally a rhetoric of emotions, especially in dealing with certain problems such as alcoholism, sexual abuse, and suicide (Ferrara 1999).

Another element in Cree selves is clearly the manner in which Crees socialize emotions. Briggs (1970) shows in her pioneering work on Inuit emotional expression – and I have found similarities with my Cree patients and informants – that emotional and personal control regulates social life. Briggs (1970, 1998) describes the Inuit term *isuma*, which involves reason and the regulation of emotional reactions. Essentially, *isuma* "refers to all functions that we think of as cerebral – mind, thought, memory, reason, sense, ideas and will" (1998, 233). In this sense, the Inuit term *isuma* is similar to the Cree word *umituunaaichikanich*. *Isuma* is regarded among the Inuit as the sacred realm of an individual's thoughts and emotions – a place only the individual has access to (Qitsualik 1998). If emotions such as anger, pain, or frustration are made apparent, then the individual in Inuit society is considered to lack *isuma* or reason (Briggs 1970). A well-developed *isuma* is the ability to act autonomously and self-sufficiently, and an adult is usually one who has *isuma* (Briggs 1987, 10). According to Cohen, *isuma* is "a way of harmonising the emotional needs of the individual with their pragmatic need for society" (1994, 36). This also seems to be relevant to my Cree informants, because both the individual and society are seen as implicated in the other. In this regard, their apparent "reticence" is better understood as an explicit attempt to reconcile the individual and the social. In other words, it is not that they do not talk and express themselves but that they are more cautious because words represent power. Darnell's argument on Cree taciturnity concords with what I am saying in that speech has little to do with the speaker and more with the listener. The one who speaks must have something to say that is not known to the listener (Darnell 1981, 57). Thus, emphasis is placed on the interaction between the individual and the other.

Among the Cree people I know verbalized emotions are also explicitly politicized communicative events because their rarity engages and demands an extremely high intensity of interaction.[7] As such, Cree people are generally very careful about expressing emotions, especially when the interaction is with non-Native observers. Silence among the Crees is often an appropriate response (Ferrara 1994; Brant 1990; Darnell 1981) to emotionally tense situations. It is not surprising that Western therapeutic practices often see the lack of emotional verbalization among the Crees as a therapeutic challenge at best and as a sign of emotional and social crippling at worst, when in fact it is a way of defusing the therapist-patient hierarchy, especially since the Western therapist often does not know the rules governing speech and silence.

Standard views among many educated Euro-Canadians, including therapists, suggest that the expression of emotion is "good" because it allows the individual to avoid somatization and neuroses.[8] In fact, a fundamental premise in psychiatry and psychotherapy is that perceptions that are verbalized can lead to an enhancement of mental health (Ferrara 1999; Pennebaker 1995). Many of my Cree patients stated that they often feel forced to talk about their feelings in other, more conventional therapies. Verbal disclosure of feelings is not perceived as a primary criterion that leads to health. In fact, "somatization" of emotions is perceived as the norm, and not something to be avoided.

The main thrust of all theories and discourse elements among Euro-Canadians suggests that verbalizing emotions is a communicative gesture whose Other is the projected self (Leavitt 1996). In other words, when someone verbalizes emotions there is often no real attempt to engage the Other. By implication, verbalization subverts the Other by incorporating the Other into the speaker's projected self. Talking openly about emotions is really a conversation with one's depersonalized, objectified, and projected self, or perhaps it is more accurate to say, with one's selves, as an attempt to reconcile different facets of various identity processes in heterogenous and highly differentiated social contexts.

This is not to say that the Crees do not acknowledge individuality; however, for the Crees, there appears to be different social and political contexts to individuality that prevent it from erupting as individualism, as described in chapter 2. My Cree informants, as with many indigenous people I have worked with, are socially and politically incorporative societies. Incorporation refers to how the production of a common group identity subsumes and may even replace an individual identity (Turner and Wertman 1977; Lanoue 1995, 7). In addition, relationships usually operate on the level of performance (e.g. cooperation in hunting and gathering tasks). What is given central importance in Western society is the development of a highly individuated self, and persons see themselves as individuals rather than as parts of relationships. Among the Crees, selfhood includes interpersonal relationships, and what exists is more of a sociocentric conception of the self.[9] The sociocentric and individualistic aspects of the Cree notion of self are not contrasting sides but seen as two parts of a balanced framework.

I have noticed with my Cree informants and patients is that the expression of emotion initiates and confirms a social responsibility.

Emotional expression is both a personal articulation and a social enactment (Lutz 1988), and it is through emotion that links between the self and social world can be clearly erected (Lyon and Barbalet 1994; Douglas 1970). Thus, there is an interplay between the individual body and the social body. The individual body refers to one's unique body image and self-identity, and the social body relates to how the body is symbolized in society and in one's social self. With the Crees, both the individual body and social body appear to be reconciled by the politics of identity:[10] in the Cree context of social incorporation, the individual body-self becomes a social body-self, and this complementarity becomes their political practice. In other words, their recent experience of being disempowered and invalidated socially and politically by Euro-Canadian society has affected their sense of corporeal embodiment,[11] and their feelings of anger and frustration are either displaced toward others, leading to violence, or self-directed, leading to self-destructive behaviour. In such conflictual situations, there may also be a resistance against their social body-self. Because of the high degree of complimentarity between the self and others in Cree society, I believe that the standard Western theory of frustration leading to displacement is invalid in the Cree case.[12] Hurting another is not so much about venting one's anger (due to impotence) at the other, as might be the case in Western societies, but another form of hurting oneself when a person feels incapable of reconciling the different and contradictory signs that define the new, political definition of "Cree-ness."

HUMAN RELATIONSHIPS

It is vital to address how my Cree patients and informants perceive human relationships, in order to better contextualize their social dynamics, their interactions with me, and their perception of me as a healer. In many ways, the Cree perception of being human is related to their model of social organization. The traditional Cree model of social relations is based on a community of individuals organized into production groups, who work together on a seasonal basis and re-form every year. The Cree social world is negotiated ad hoc within known limits rather than by individuals adhering to a precise set of values and practices. In terms of kinship beliefs, Cree people often refer to each other by relationship terms that imply communality and cooperation. Within the context of self-as-community, human relationships are formed for pragmatic reasons, to help maintain patterns of cooperation and shared residential histories. The Shamattawa Crees described by D.H. Turner (1978, 9) show similar features, especially with regard to their way of structuring the world in such a way that pragmatic flexibility is given free rein but occurs within a structured framework, so that flexibility in the formation of relationships never threatens the construction and stability of the collective.

The development of relationships with others is integral not only for the evolution of community life but for the individual's personal growth; these are interdependent. An individual's problems affect both his personal health and that of the community. The Crees tend to avoid labelling a person as "deviant" or as a problematic individual because this would only foster the person's marginalization from the community (Preston 1991). Given what I have said about the Cree self being reciprocally embedded in the collective, the "failure" of an individual – in hunting, in social relationships, and in what we call psychological equilibrium – is also the failure of the community. Instead, steps are taken that are believed to favour the reintegration of that person back into his/her social networks (Preston 1991; Ferrara 1996). For example, the first session I had with a Cree "bushman"[13] in art therapy (Ferrara 1996) was also attended by his three siblings and his community worker. They were all determined to help this individual address his "deviant" behaviour, that is, his alcoholism and acts of vandalism. They were also present to assess my effectiveness in facilitating this person's healing process. If I represented a negative influence in any way or was uncooperative with their approach, I would have been seen as an outside source who does not promote community strength, and therefore I would weaken their effectiveness in helping this individual through his troubles. In terms of Cree relations with Euro-Canadians, Tanner (1999) defines it as an "exclusionist" approach, in that they remain guarded as they consider the possibility of incorporating outside innovations into their existing ways of doing things. Their subsequent perception of me was as a non-threatening individual because I intervened little and let them do most of the talking. As therapy progressed, they eventually considered me an effective healer/therapist.

As I have witnessed, the Crees develop acquaintances initially, assess the potentialities of the relationship, and then relate to the person according to what he or she does rather than what the person says or claims; status symbols and identity markers familiar to Euro-Canadians, such as clothes, jewellery, possessions in general, "good" manners, etc., are irrelevant to Cree interaction. Crees are relatively insensitive to our rhetorics of the self, especially self-produced and self-referential rhetoric. For instance, I was initially perceived as a "whiteman-outsider-therapist," and only when I "proved" myself by facilitating successful treatments was I accepted and considered a "healer" or *minwachihiwaw*.[14] In the past, Cree models for healing were more male-centred because healing rituals were usually conducted by male elders, but female healers are becoming more common, some are actually running healing circles and sweat lodges,[15] once the prerogative of male healers. I worked with a Cree female healer in a halfway house for Native male prisoners and she conducted healing circles and sweat lodges with clients and co-workers. Many of my informants and patients believe that a healer's effectiveness rests not on their gender but on their ability to open a closed mind and heart. In fact, most social categories among the Crees are not coded for gender. For example, while in the bush, men usually go hunting while the women stay in the wigwam (tent) to clean, prepare the food, and take care of the small children. However, it is believed that women could go hunting and the men could stay in the wigwam, which is sometimes the case. Thus, there is no highly specialized division of labour, nor are there gender-specific roles.

The difference with interaction with my non-Native patients is that the Crees are more sensitive to what I do and relatively insensitive to the status differences that frame doctor-patient relationships in Euro-Canadian society. Another difference is that there are no ideologically sanctioned categories for the Crees. My work is legitimated not by a particular ideology of power but because the Quebec Cree community has gradually developed faith in art therapy intervention, and this faith became an influential factor in the successful treatments that followed. My Cree patients find rhetorical coherency in the space provided by the art therapy context, and because art therapy (and the art therapist) is initially silent it is easier for individuals to incorporate me into their notion of the generalized Other, which concords well with their notion of the autonomous self as incorporating others. Thus, art therapy succeeds among the Crees because it is consonant with Cree cultural principles about the nature of the individual in relation to the community and about the nature of healing.

In brief, the Crees usually have a "wait and see" attitude before deciding to adopt or reject Western elements. Again, this is very suggestive of the weakness of ideological conditioning. This is not to say that the past and in particular, past experience are ignored. On the contrary, all knowledge is experientially produced, evaluated, and, literally, embodied, to such an extent that knowledge is always keyed to the individual and his or her existential contingencies, and this is why rhetoric divorced from action is largely ignored.

4

Cree Mythopoetic Thought

Before developing my analysis on mythopoetic thought as I witnessed it among my Cree informants and patients, and how this relates to the self and to healing, I would like to elaborate on their process of reality construction, how they seem to integrate knowledge and experience, and show how these elements influence the formation of their notion of self and vice versa. Cree interaction patterns, their narrative and emotional discourses, and the way they perceive humans and animals illustrate their culturally patterned ways of reality construction.

I have noticed that the Crees often invoke combinations of the so-called rational-empirical dimensions of life and what we call mythical aspects in a semi-sacred, semi-secular fashion. Myth is conceived as logical and empirical, though its meanings are fluid and its narratives non-linear. During the past twelve years of clinical work and fieldwork with the Crees in northern Quebec, I have been in the process of re-thinking my own ways of knowing and understanding human behaviour, using the Cree thought system.[1] This is not to say that I am a "wanna-be Cree," but having had such exposure to their ways, I am in essence acculturating into the Cree culture (as I know it) by adopting ways that feel relevant to my own experience and values. I have moved beyond perceiving the Cree understanding of things as merely a diverse cultural construction of reality and I am now in the process of using it to better understand my being and the environment I am a part of. Personally, I always felt that the Euro-Canadian thought system in which I was socialized was limiting, reducing experience to a singular modality or a particular classified slot.

In the Euro-Canadian society that I am a part of, mythopoetic thought is often seen as illogical, as producing statements or stories that are untestable or blatantly false, like fairy tales. This perception demonstrates ideological limits that recognize only particular kinds of logic. The symbolic aspect of Cree reality makes the intangible seem tangible, the mythical not mystical, and reality grounded and balanced. I have found coherence in the Cree perspective on drawing attention to polysemic relational unities rather than focusing on simple dualities. Among my Cree informants I have noticed that metaphor is used to explore the potential relationship between two things, such as between human and animal, rather than the figurative, realized relationship. According to my informants, their reality set is not "mythopoetic" or "symbolic," it is simply connected to their environment and their everyday lived experiences. From their perspective, the knowledge and poetics that stem from myth provide great insight because they are seen as lived reality while at the same time they conserve the power of myth to metonymically link aspects of experience and thought that are not causally linked by rational and positivistic logic.

MYTHOPOETIC THOUGHT

Cree reality is characterized by a perception of the world in which humans, animals, and nature all play significant roles in transmitting knowledge orally, by rote and/or by re-enactment in language, art, myth, and ritual. A significant amount of education occurs within the family, and it is characterized by an accent on first-hand experience and direct observation, as well as by active non-interference on the parents' part (Berry and Bennett 1992, 75; Brant 1990). My informants unanimously said that children are allowed and encouraged to explore the world on their own terms. Such an approach is believed to foster the development of qualities of independence, equality, perseverance, and respect, which are valued by Cree society (Berry and Bennett 1992, 76). This type of knowledge is highly contextualized because of the intimate contact between individuals and things. It also fosters a gradual development of levels of abstraction, which contrasts against the cognitive values of de-contextualization taught in the present school system (Berry and Bennett 1992), where knowledge is usually enforced upon the individual and first-hand experience in acquiring knowledge is rarely emphasized. As a Cree informant stated, the Euro-Canadian educational system depersonalizes the learning process and detracts from a communal way of learning and living. The values taught in the Euro-Canadian schools contribute to alienation and the isolation of the person within his/her environment, according to the Crees.

Scollon and Scollon's (1979, 1981) model of narrative discourse and bush consciousness of the Athabaskans in Alberta is useful here in understanding the reality set of the Cree people I have met and worked with. In Cree views of reality, the trait of non-interference in others' affairs, including that of children, is extended to include non-negotiation of personal intersubjective reality, which refers to the internal world of the self. In other words, an individual's inner reality is considered a private realm to which only the individual has access. An individual exists in an unspoken state of truce with others, and his/her thoughts are not scrutinized nor questioned. The individual is a central, organizing trait or aspect of "bush consciousness," which is a general term relating to the reality set or mode of thinking of many aboriginal groups. There is a high degree of respect for the individuality of others and careful guarding of one's own individuality (Scollon and Scollon 1981, 15). Individual autonomy can only be obtained to the extent that it is granted to one by others. Thus, among the Crees, individual autonomy may be viewed as a social product (Scollon and Scollon 1981). The Cree sense of self is constructed with a definite view of the other. Although it appears as a sociocentric conception of self, there is also another dimension: nature. Thus, as discussed in chapter 2, a more relevant category in terms of Cree psychology of individuality would be "ecocentrism," with "eco-" encompassing the full environment, which includes others and non-human beings (Stairs 1992, 119–20). Just as the collective is implicated in the construction of the self, land and animals also constitute dimensions of the Cree self. Becoming a person entails participating in an interrelationship with the physical environment as well as with the social world.[2] This indigenous form of individuality allows for multiple meanings and definitions of self, which relate more easily to Cree mythologic.

I have noticed among the Cree people that knowledge is formulated in concrete and pragmatic terms, and it is thus highly personal and idiosyncratic and keyed to individual experiences. It is conceived as the result of the individual's personal experience. Bush consciousness is characterized by non-intervention in others' lives, and foreign elements are integrated into the reality set only if they do not threaten an individual's personal view. "Respect" for others is not a moral value as it is among Euro-Canadians. Instead, it is an acknowledgment that the self is inextricably implicated in the surrounding world, be it physical or social; harming others or the environment is harming oneself. For instance, while I was in the bush gathering berries for the first time with an informant, Sid, I was tempted to pick all the berries in sight. Sid was quickly attuned to my apparent greediness, and he asked me to just watch him. He picked berries from each plant he saw and only from those within his reach, along our path. I carefully watched Sid and picked a few berries myself. The second time we went berrying, I asked Sid why he never picked from the first plants we saw, and he responded, "the first berries you see should be respected and left alone just in case they are the last ones in the bush. They belong to the animals." He also told me that berries are viewed as *iiyiyuu miichim*, forest food and part of the pure spiritual domain of the forest.

This experience is also suggestive of the emphasis placed on an individual's ability to construct knowledge and integrate it with the sum of past knowledge, including knowledge that comes from the collective-in-the-self and knowledge that comes from nature-in-the-self. Knowledge is not enforced upon people. Rather, the individual should interpret a given experience when ready and not before (Scollon and Scollon 1981; Preston 2002). The experiential interpretation of events attaches a subjective meaning to reality. According to Ghostkeeper, Cree "traditional" knowledge is in contrast to Western scientific knowledge, which accentuates that objective interpretation reveals the scientific meaning of reality (Ghostkeeper 1996). I disagree with Ghostkeeper's approach because he constructs a dichotomous relationship between Cree and Western notions. Nonetheless, his dichotomy of (Plains) Cree and Western worldviews is theoretical and political rather than absolute. Most of my Cree informants do not view the differences in this fashion. They do not necessarily discount Western ways, and will adopt ways that they feel are effective and necessary, such as biomedical treatments.

Many Crees believe that the experiential basis of knowledge is ecological (and inherently spiritual), and knowledge is adapted to perception and imagination, where Western scientific knowledge is removed from them. Mythological knowledge and certain forms of understanding based on empirical reality are valid, say the Crees, even though many Westerners usually discount them because in a modern world driven by technology, science seems to provide the absolute authority for all knowledge.

Lévi-Strauss's (1966, 14) comparative analysis of "traditional" knowledge and scientific knowledge is similar to Ghostkeeper's approach. According to Lévi-Strauss, "traditional" knowledge approaches the physical world in concrete terms, recognizing its sensible qualities, while the Western form approaches it in abstract terms, recognizing its formal properties (269). Traditional knowledge is defined by Lévi-Strauss as analogical thought, where analogical relationships between an individual's life and the life of nature are established instantaneously. Although this comparative analysis may seem too black and white, what is significant is that these different perspectives fundamentally determine the type of knowledge that is obtained, and each is endowed with originality, internal coherence, and intellectual integrity (Lévi-Strauss 1966). Lévi-Strauss underlines Giambattista Vico's idea that myths underlie the cognitive structures and processes that allow humans to make sense of the perceived environment (Danesi 1993, 49), and this view appears pertinent in describing Cree reality. Because in Cree reality knowledge is represented in experiential terms, it is automatically metonymized when communicated to others.

This definition of the Cree knowledge system shows how it is closely linked to the physical environment as well as to the metaphysical dimension. Among the Crees there is no apparent distinction made between the physical and metaphysical dimensions. Thus, contrary to Leach's (1976) perspective, mythologic thought, for the Crees, does not necessarily conflict with the empirical rules of the physical environment. The Cree use of mythical symbolism is often directed toward some logic of practical, social, or environmental knowledge (Scott 1996, 70–1). The coherence of myths depends much more on a unity of feeling than on logical rules. Many of my Cree informants believe that reality is constructed and not discovered, and its construction is a continuous process. As Lyne noted, "My grandparents always told me that we learn through experience and the more experience we have the more knowledge." She then added: "to understand the present we also need to listen to the stories from our past." Myth allows more truths to be "constructed" because it works on metonymy, not metaphor. Myths express images that provide a source of knowledge. The social context of mythopoesis is that the myths are circulated among and between others as tokens of identity, and they are used as tools to arrange and interpret life experiences and help make transcendental realities more coherent.

Cree mythologic thought can be best described as "a symbolic process resting on images that are not simply reducible to verbal articulations of experience" (Ewing 1990, 268). For example, during one of my bush experiences, a Cree informant mentioned that he hunts the animal only when the animal is ready. Moreover, the hunter will wait until the animal tells him he/she is ready to be given to him and the nourishing substance of the animal is received as a gift (Ingold 1996; Scott 1996; Tanner 1979; Feit 1973). Many of my informants, both male and female, expressed their belief that animals are sensitive to any lack of respect shown by humans. As Tanner writes, "According to many Cree hunters, the relationship between human beings and animals cannot be understood solely in terms of an ecosystem model that only looks at materialistic interchanges among life forms; for them, there are moral and spiritual aspects to be considered as well" (1999, 126). The interpersonal dialogue between humans and animals is metaphysical and the mythopoetic dimension is that qualities of personhood are assigned to humans, animals, spirits, and certain geophysical agents, such as the wind, the earth, and trees (Ingold 1996, 131). There is a poetic sensibility, a poetic logic in Cree discourse in that they seek aid from their imagination to explain the transcendental and make sense of it. Their narratives and myths are not only an embroidery of reality but a way of coping with it. According to Vico, the purpose of such "poetic wisdom" is for an individual to create accounts and myths that manifest his/her perception of the world, and in this process the individual is also constructing his or her self.[3]

Mythological thought, or what Lévi-Strauss preferred to call mythical thought, works with images and events that are meaningful while providing aesthetic satisfaction and helping people understand reality (Lévi-Strauss 1966). I found a parallel in my Cree patients' use of myths in art therapy and Lévi-Strauss's explanation of the use of myth narratives in a ritual context, specifically a curing rite among the Cuna of Panama. Lévi-Strauss (1963, 188) claims that the myth narrative permits the patient, who is undergoing a shamanistic curing ritual, to cope with a psycho-physiological trauma by providing a type of "objective correlative" for the patient's repressed and inarticulate experience of trauma with a metaphorically induced parallelism between the myth world and the patient's own experience. According to Lévi-Strauss, during the ritual the inexpressible is sensed. Similarly, my Cree patients often refer to myths and folktales to help make sense of the conflicts or traumatic experiences that have affected them, and this process somehow helps them to reframe and rearticulate their life experiences, which leads to feeling more grounded and secure. A Cree legend I have often heard is about a poor little orphan girl who was abandoned by her family. As she was about to die of cold and starvation, a grey bird with a white head, referred to as Whiskey-jack (a Canada Jay), landed beside her. He proposed to save her if she would promise to give him food for the rest of her life. She promised and then Whiskey-jack grew before her eyes, told the girl to climb on his back, and took her to a new camp, where they fed and clothed her. Everyone respected her because she had a powerful guardian spirit. The girl kept her promise and fed her feathered friend and she lived for many years, until she had snow-white hair, like the bird. As one of my patients noted, this legend was told to him by an elder who had noticed the young boy's feelings of helplessness and despair, in hopes to inspire him. The patient told me that he believed it was a good legend to share with my other patients who were feeling the same emotions he had felt.

ANIMAL-DOCTOR RELATIONSHIPS

In my fieldwork with the Crees, an example of their narrative discourse is their description of animal-doctor conversations, which are considered a very important component of the self. Metonymic and metaphoric associations are reflected in Cree animal-doctor relationships, which are an integral element of Cree reality. A way of life of the past that is considered a source of well-being by many of my informants is contact with "animal-doctors," an English term used by the Crees to describe animals who confer messages and power on people. Animal-doctor discourse may be seen as a new form of the traditional relationship to the past used as an instrument of persuasion that both modifies and maintains the Cree social formation (Tanner 1997; Scott 1996); in other words, this discourse has important social implications. It is an instrument of ancestral knowledge that modifies Cree social formation because the knowledge of an animal also gives a person the ability to affect the behaviour of people around him. It maintains Cree social structure because it is considered by many as a cultural template that is a mainstay in Cree society

(Tanner 1997), although it has been heavily modified by the vicissitudes of modernization and can thus be seen as only a partial representation of the past (Lanoue 1999). In other words, these individuals are reconstructing the past and taking what they need in order to develop a more balanced sense of self. By maintaining their belief in animal-doctors, which is a commonly shared belief, according to my informants, there is a link to the "past" ways of life that define the Crees as a collectivity. It also reflects the characteristic trait of Cree mythic discourse that encourages the maintenance of harmony with the natural and spiritual worlds.

For many Cree individuals, usually male,[4] the basis of Cree identity is the psychological sensibility to "conversations" with animal-doctors, and these are as private as they are intensely moving. Women are not excluded from this relationship to animals, and their role entails "the maintenance of the proper negotiation between the spirit world and the world of the Cree" (Adelson 2000, 69). In the bushcamp, both women and men are expected to demonstrate the same respect toward animals (Adelson 2000). The men usually hand the women their hunting bags, which includes their kill, and the women unpack it in silence (Tanner 1979). The hunter who has made a significant kill (eg. bear, moose, caribou, or beaver) does not openly brag about his success. Although they are proud, there is a taboo placed on boasting. Women help the men lay out their kill for others to admire; their intense curiosity, excitement, and pride are expressed non-verbally by laying out particular parts of the game (Tanner 1979). According to my informants, the silence that occurs during the return of the kill is primarily to demonstrate respect toward the animals, who gave up their lives for them. Respect for the animals is a constant throughout the hunting experience – from the initial encounter, the kill, the return to the camp, and the cleaning of the killed animal, to the feast that follows. As described by Tanner (1979, 180), these ritualized aspects assure the continuity of the animal world, as well as that of the people.

A forty-six-year-old female patient related to her role as a woman in the bush as being essential to maintaining a balance between "this world and the spirit world of the animals." She described this after drawing figure 4.1, which depicts how she would prepare a fire to smoke goose meat. As I noticed while in the bush camp, all the women present, young and old, were keeping busy maintaining a clean dwelling in the wigwam, and they derived great pride from the fish they had hung to be smoked. Many Crees believe that if the

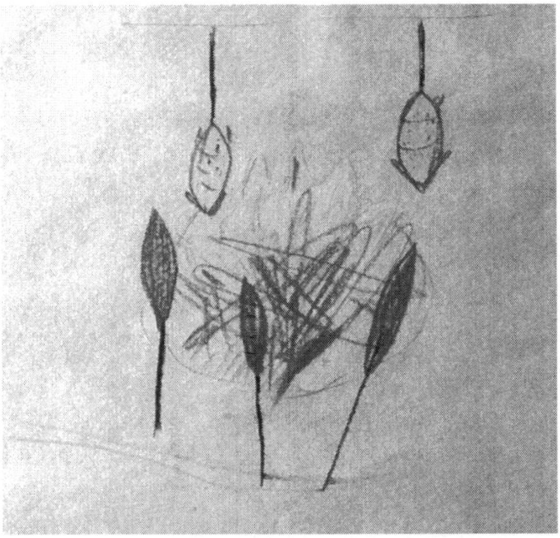

Figure 4.1 Smoking goose meat

dwelling is not clean then the animals will not want to enter it because it is unworthy of their presence (Adelson 2000, 69). As Scott also notes, when a goose is killed it is later received as a guest into the lodge by the women of the hunter's household, again illustrating the important role a woman plays in the bush (1996, 82).

The communication between humans and animals is silent. This interpersonal dialogue is "integral to the total process of social life wherein both human and animal persons are constituted with their particular identities and purposes" (Ingold 1996, 131). According to Cree perspective, the social interaction between humans and animals is made possible because animals live in social groups or communities similar to those of humans, yet they remain superior to humans (Tanner 1979, 137–8) because, for example, they survive without tools and language. Through conversations and interactions, humans receive the nourishing substance of animals as a gift. There are overlapping dimensions of resemblance and difference among the categories of humans, animals, and the interactions between them, which are also reciprocally defining: "the existence of particular modes of interaction is based on the understood character of the animal; reciprocally, the character of the animal is built up in terms of the role it plays in human social life" (Brightman 1993, 34).

Contact with animal-doctors is an intensely private experience for many Crees and is therefore difficult to study. It appears inherently dangerous, since animals are believed to be superior to humans as a class of living entities yet both are part of a network of reciprocating persons (Scott 1989, 195). Animals are seen as superior in the sense that they can be role models for humans, and so, respectful activity toward the animals is enhanced. When respect is demonstrated toward the animals, then the animals are more ready to give themselves to the hunters. The sharing of animal gifts among hunters and their households is another important dimension of respect for the animals (Scott 1996, 82). Both of these propositions allude to the human-animal reciprocity and social-ecological principles of Cree knowledge.

When these animal-doctor relationships are disclosed in the clinical setting, images of the animal often appear in artwork, usually with the intention, conscious or unconscious, of articulating and recording a person's dreams of the animal or to describe a past experience with an animal-doctor. Although this information on animal-doctors may be considered fragmentary and problematic because it surfaces mostly in a therapeutic setting and not in a "normal" context, I believe it provides an enriching ethnographic account that should not be dismissed. Descriptions of animal-doctor relationships may be the Cree individuals' reconstructions of the past that allow them to face the future. In this form of narrative construction, they may be using a motif of the return to the forest. However, I believe that the therapeutic space becomes an appropriate context for revealing personal engagement of a present institution that is not normally discussed openly.

Many Cree people experience modern animal species and their attributes as icons of the proto-animal characters in myth, resembling them in name and physical and behavioural traits (Brightman 1993, 57).[5] My Cree informants also believe that there was a time when the proto-animal giants of myth hunted and ate people. Through time these animals transformed and evolved into their present form, yet their power remains. These proto-animal giants of myth are usually positively portrayed and are said to have given to humans the use of fire, tools, and other aspects of culture.

When an individual becomes possessed and believes he has the power to eat other humans, this usually occurs in the form of dream visits by the cannibalistic spirit referred to by the Crees, like many Algonquians, as "Windigo" or *atuush* (Marano 1982).[6] Unlike the proto-animal giants of myth, *atuush* is monstrous and ethically sub-human.

I have not actually met anyone who experienced the Windigo phenomenon first-hand, but I discussed it with individuals who had seen it in others. In these cases, the victim was usually treated by a shaman, who administered Cree medicines from plants and trees. I was told the individuals were not marginalized, mainly because the people around them believe their condition is real. In Ridington's comparison of the Athapaskan and Algonquian belief in a cannibal monster, he shows that the Athapaskan belief in Wechuge and the Algonquian belief in Windigo are similar, and that these beliefs are very ingrained in the values of each group: "Both Algonquians and Athapaskans share a common mythical background of belief in giant person-eating animals, a transformative culture hero, and some form of association between supernatural power and the eating of creatures who are sentient and volitional" (1990, 162). The expression "windigo" refers to a cannibalistic monster or ghost that haunts human settlements, and it has been reported by a number of authors (Jenness 1977; Marano 1982; D.H. Turner 1978), who have often considered this phenomenon a psychological weakness and a culturally patterned form of psychosis (Ridington 1990, 160). The person possessed by the Windigo spirit acts like a cannibal monster, with a compulsive desire and craving for human flesh (Ridington 1990, 180). Windigo behaviour is believed to be genuine by the afflicted individual and by those around him.

Dreams are important vehicles by which humans communicate with animal-doctors and keep alive a mythopoetic approach to knowledge. Images are found in dreams and they may be kept as private experience and without word form (Preston 1982, 305). As Hallowell claims in his description of the role of dreams in the Ojibwa culture, which is also relevant to Cree people, "imaginative processes linked with traditional values play a vital role in psychocultural adaptation" (1966, 271). Dreams are also interpreted by Cree individuals as "actual experiences of the self" (Hallowell 1966, 271). Many informants told me that their continuing belief in sorcery is one reason Cree people place emphasis on their dreams. Several Cree men and women have told me how they use their dreams and powers to help each other through illness, other troubles, and to hunt better to feed their loved ones.[7] Dream revelations are often used to predict animal behaviour and improve hunting success (Niezen 1998).

Essentially, animals are ascribed intellectual, emotional, and spiritual characteristics that in many respects parallel those of humans

(Tanner 1979; Scott 1989; Brightman 1993). It is important to point out, as noted by Preston (2002), Tanner (1979), and Scott (1989), that animals are not necessarily anthropomorphized natural forces, which would assume the primacy of human beings; this is categorically rejected by many Cree people. From the Cree perspective, both animals and humans are different forms of personhood, sharing a common existential status (Ingold 1996). Crees also believe animals have dual forms of existence, the physical and the transcendental. The physical attributes, that is, arms, legs, fur, and face, have evolved through time, but the spirit form remains the same. Humans connect with the atemporal dimension, that is, the transcendental spirit form of the animal and not the corporeal dimension. Thus, humans make contact with the invisible rather than the visible realm. Cree men who want to be successful hunters seek knowledge from animals by contacting this invisible dimension:

> In certain ritual contexts, the identity of the hunter merges radically with that of the animal, a merging accomplished through body-spirit reciprocity. … In a dream, the goose may be a guardian of the hunter's power and essence and may protect him from sorcery. Throughout his life, the hunter receives the gift of geese, and at a hunter's death, it is often a goose that represents his soul on its journey from this life. … The hunter's experience of animals as interpretants of his essential self renders all the more poignant the inevitable separation of hunter from prey, and all the more compelling the morality that joins them in the reciprocity of life-giving and life-taking. The transcendence of this tension … is the experience of the sacred. (Scott 1996, 84)

This analysis of animal-human reciprocity illustrates how animal-human relationships become instrumental in the metonymic construction of self (Lanoue 2000), which essentially relates to how my Cree patients incorporate their experiences with animal-doctors in their construction of a new sense of self, especially in relation to the embodiment of the self-in-nature.

Similar to some Northern Athapaskan peoples (Desgent and Lanoue 2001; Mills 1986; Goulet 1994a, 1994b; Moore and Wheelock 1990), my Cree informants also believe animals have special abilities that they depend upon to live, and they give humans only the powers they no longer need. "An animal chooses someone to receive these leftover powers, a person who has treated the animals with respect" (Goulet 1994a, 159). With these powers, one's life is enhanced. For instance, hunting prowess is a sign of successful contact with animal-doctors (Tanner 1979). One becomes familiar with his/her animal helper through a personal and private encounter with the animal. Animals are believed to understand a hunter's state of mind and they give themselves only to people with whom they had made contact through dreams (Tanner 1979).

Animal-human "dialogue," which is silent, is considered much more significant than dialogue with humans. As Scott explains, "animal behaviour can become a model for human relations" (1989, 198). Human conversation is of a much lower order because humans play only a small part in the universe and they must use words, learn language explicitly, etc. Emotions are engaged more with animal-doctors, and emotional extremes are avoided because they upset the equilibrium of the relationship. Many Cree people believe that the public manifestation of strong emotions that lead to social conflict also cause animals to cease contact with humans. Some of my patients, as well as other informants, have said that the loss of contact with the animal-doctors and the lack of harmonious relationships between animals and humans are the root of many of the problems facing the Crees today. Some Cree elders I spoke with believe the animal-doctors have retreated into the bush or have gone away. These elders also feel that they are now in a state of disequilibrium because the connection is lost.

Animal-doctors or helpers may be more familiar to the elders than to the younger generation in Cree society. However, I have met with young people who have had encounters with animal-doctors. These young individuals have lived in the bushcamp more than some of their peers, and they have also maintained close ties with their elders. As among the Dene Tha (Slave) (Goulet 1994b; Mills 1986; Sharp 1988; Smith 1973), some Cree parents continue to encourage their children to go to the bush to find their animal-helper. In fact, some interpersonal, interfamilial conflicts are still handled in part by recourse to animal-doctors. An example of this process among the Crees was a six-year-old boy who was in residential treatment for his anti-social behaviour. While in treatment in Montreal, 750 miles away from his northern Cree village, this child developed suicidal tendencies. His parents lived in the bush throughout the year. When I met with them and his Cree community worker, they discussed this boy's need to return to the bush to find his animal helper. With this in mind, as his primary therapist, I made the recommendation to the agency that he be removed from treatment and the school system and that he return to the bush. My recommendation went against the agency's regulation to maintain the child in the school system. This regulation is also imposed on the people in the northern communities, and many Cree people feel that the children are forced to attend school and often miss out on the bushlife. This case exemplifies how this regulation could become a source of tension. While in the bush with his family, this boy's suicidal tendencies disappeared. According to his family members, the child's quest was complete as he connected with the natural and animal worlds.[8]

Thus, in contrast to the Sekani, an Athapaskan group in northwest Canada studied by Lanoue (1999), many Crees in Quebec continue to initiate contact with their modern spiritual embodiments, and their relationships to animals have involved profound connections that empower them. My patient Tom described an encounter he had with a caribou, initially in a dream and then in the bush. He symbolized this experience in figure 4.2, which he drew after his encounter. He took two full sessions to complete this piece, from which he derived a great sense of pride. Tom placed it in his room as a reminder of his encounter and the gift he received from the caribou. He expressed that this interaction actually made him a better hunter and also put him more in touch with ancestral spirits, depicted in figures 4.3 and 4.4. These drawings illustrate the day spirit and night spirit of the bush camp, respectively, and they both represent ancestors of this particular bushcamp. Tom believed that his dreams had direct implications on the subsequent, successful bush activities, both his own and that of his kin. Also, Tom said that the caribou helped him to connect with his ancestors, especially after his father had passed away. The caribou gave him the strength to carry on as a skillful bushman. According to Adelson's (2000) description of animal spirit, *mischinaakw,* Tom's hunting success was because the animal spirit of the caribou lived within him. In one of our sessions, Tom had referred to *pihkutiskwaauu,* "the Lady Spirit of the Caribou," which according to Cree animal taxonomy belongs to the highest order of spirits in the hierarchy of animal, human, and supernatural beings (Adelson 2000, 69).[9]

Tanner (1997) recently noted that the younger generations of the Crees may want non-Cree people to believe that animal helpers do not exist as they did before. They simply refuse to talk about their encounters in their private world because they see this as a violation.[10] They develop this form of resistance because their cultural beliefs have been

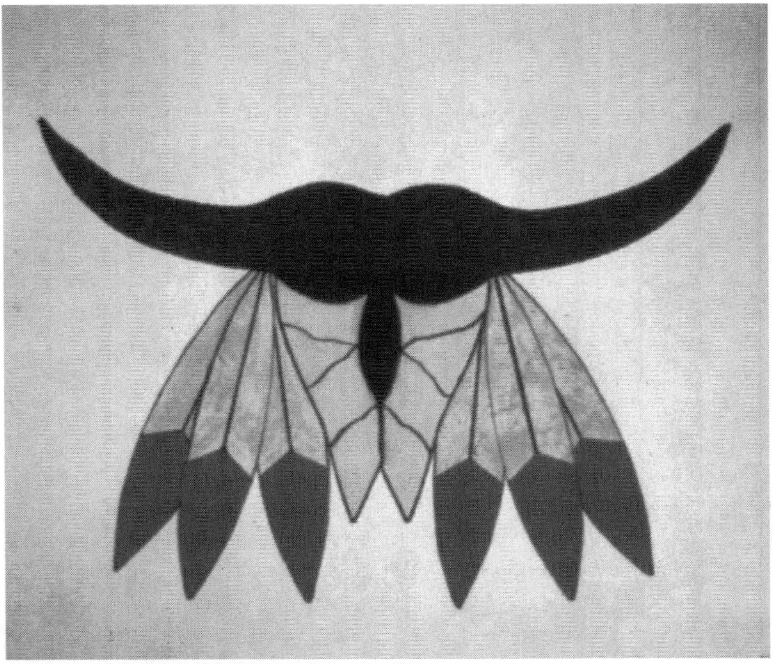

Figure 4.2 Tom's caribou

threatened and some magico-religious customs, such as this one, have been invalidated or criticized by whites. Although the associations of people to the bush may now be much weaker than in the past and this particular way of life may be practised by a Cree minority, Tanner (1997) believes human-animal-doctor relationships remain common in Cree society today despite the reluctance to talk about them.

In addition, the Cree individuals I have worked with may have chosen the motif of the return to the forest to regain a sense of self-worth. This motif plays a significant role in the image the Crees want to create and project to the Euro-Canadian world. I believe the motif also alludes to the problem of hierarchy: hierarchy is usually perceived as having a vertical and social orientation, while the return to the forest is horizontal and spatial. It may not be that surprising that the impossibility of resolving the "vertical" conflict between Euro-Canadians and Crees is projected "horizontally" onto the "friendly" forest, where, without a constant struggle for recognition, individuals feel more competent (Lanoue 1989, 1990). Perhaps what Crees would like non-Cree people to see is that they identify themselves with

Figure 4.3 Tom's day spirit

nature and animals because it elicits a positive image of themselves. However, many Cree people feel that they do not necessarily need to "return" to the bush because they feel they never left it. They believe they are in the process of maintaining certain cultural patterns that they are combining with selected Euro-Canadian traits.

This type of experiential interpretation of behaviour invokes a subjective meaning of reality that creates an individual mythical space. In this space, things that cannot normally be experienced become visible, especially the transcendental spirit form of the animal (Lanoue 1999, 2). Other aspects of the Cree self are also instrumental in their projection of this image. It is important to note that Cree individuals only explain their encounters with animal-doctors to me once I have shown my understanding of their cultural ways and when they feel that their beliefs are not threatened. This suggests that these contemporary narratives differ from the traditional narratives that describe the mythical past because there is a much stronger element of self-affirmation in contemporary narratives.

Figure 4.4 Tom's night spirit

Even if in the context of art therapy this discourse involves the creation and projection of positive images, it often entails the expression of imagery that is highly emotionally charged for the Crees. Although the narratives may be structured in part because of the therapist-patient relationship (Schafer 1981; Besnier 1990), they are also expressive of the implicit hierarchical dimension of Cree speech, which, as I have pointed out, is somewhat problematical for the Crees. These narratives probably reflect the same ambiguity. Because animal-doctor–human relationships are said to take place only in the transcendental dimension created by the metonymic shifts of mythologic, the narratives describing these relationships take on a mythic quality. By transcendental, I mean that the animals do not actually talk but communicate with and confer power to the Cree individuals by metaphysical means, as we would describe it. Cree people say they "just know." The narrated stories are understood to have originated as discourse about actual events, either related by eye-witnesses and handed down through the generations or learned about in dreams (Brightman 1993, 57). They are not subject to verification or measured and evaluated in terms of experiential or empirical reality, and so are reified and present themselves to their Cree creators as impersonal and "objectively" true, thus reinforcing Cree identity choices.

Through this mythic form of thought, the individual constitutes behaviour by reference to mythical guidelines. In fact, my informants say that myths address important truths about the human experience in society. As "true" statements, these myths generate meaning and coherence of certain life experiences that may otherwise be inexplicable, such as the conflict of identity choices facing the Crees. The process of objectification of these narratives allows them to become highly individual, because what is "objectively" true is "universally" true, and what is "universally" true must be true for each individual. Because these narratives are believed to be based on lived experiences, they become more meaningful for each individual. As Preston explains, "ambiguity and unpredictability…are inherent in the personal meanings that are symbolized in the narratives." Art and myth are appealing because they utilize an aspect of ambiguity, and Cree narration helps reduce such ambiguity through a precise and sensitive understanding of the whole context (2002, 76).

A case example is Luke's experience of killing his first goose. When he turned eleven years old, he went into the bush and had a "conversation" with a goose. According to Luke, who happened to be in the final stage of therapy with me at this time, the goose told him he was ready to be killed by him. The goose then flew overhead and Luke shot him down. For many Crees, the first killing of a goose by an adolescent boy symbolizes his entrance into manhood. Luke was aware of this and he was thrilled about this important life experience. He had always heard about it since his parents are among the few who still live in the bush eight to nine months of the year. Luke was eager to attend art therapy to tell me about his experience and to draw it (figure 4.5). He also described the ritual that followed in his bushcamp, with the goose head displayed in the centre of the wigwam (figure 2.2), and his family feasting and eating the roasted goose.

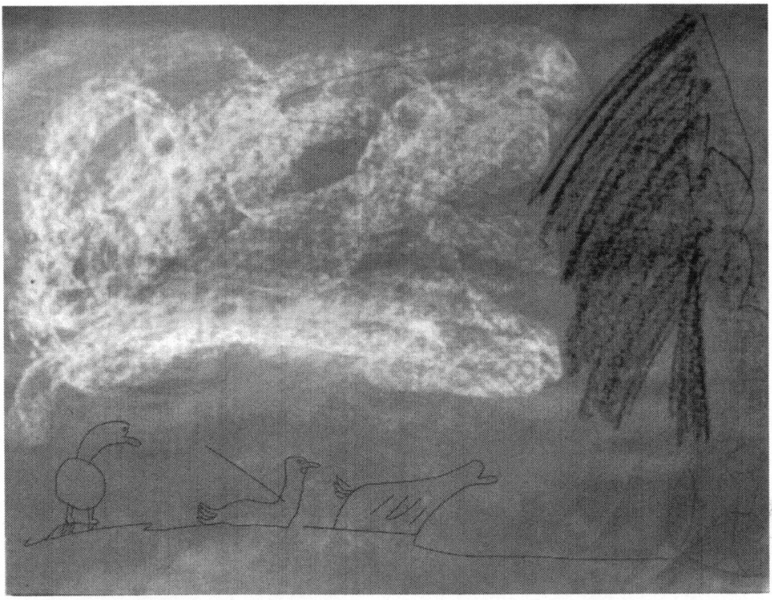

Figure 4.5 Luke's killing of the goose
Luke drew himself in the blind in the bottom right-hand corner with the goose he had killed.

Luke's experience characterizes the transcendental type of conversation between humans and animals and the reciprocity of life-giving and life-taking (Scott 1996). On the experiential level, Luke subjectively engaged in the metaphysical reality of human-animal conversation, making the mythical seem concrete. The experience was embodied and then a narrative was created. In art therapy, the narrative was verbalized and visualized in a form of a drawing. Luke's sense of self became inseparable from the narrative that encapsulated the diverse aspects of his personality into a single meta-narrative. What was generated through this narrative was a public self that was accepted by his family and peers, after many years of not having been allowed in the bush due to aggressive behaviour and having been shifted between twelve different foster homes. It also highlighted how he had gained self-acceptance and understanding as a Cree individual. He had also accepted his hearing impairment, as he wore his hearing aid on a regular basis, thus diminishing his frustration and subsequent aggression. Luke was definitely empowered by this animal encounter. After two and a half years of residential treatment, Luke returned home to attend school and remain active in bush life rituals and activities.

NARRATIVE DISCOURSE

Cree mythopoetic reality involves using narratives to communicate one's perception and understanding of the world. The narratives that surface in art therapy, whether evoked by the artwork created by the patient or not, become vehicles for the individual's search for and definition of self. In both clinical and non-clinical settings with the Crees, I have noticed an interplay between speech acts and image acts[11] in their discourse, which often entails the expression of narratives. Bakewell defines image acts as actions, and as visible speech acts that are not marginal to human communication (1998, 30). The images created and the body gestures of the Cree people and patients I have worked with are as important as their speech utterances, if not more so, since non-verbal repertoires are more common than verbal in Cree society. In art therapy, the images become a source of knowledge for the patients. Narratives expressed in a mythic form become experiential knowledge, which is retained because the narratives are meaningful to the patient.

According to Preston (2002), Cree narration serves to report meaningful events that may sometimes be remembered more as visual images than as words. Cree names are also quite descriptive. As Rob eloquently explained, "My name is *Naeepuuskumkawppaow,* which was my great grandfather's Cree name. I am not the only one who holds his name. It means 'Caribou Standing,' looking over his shoulder at the herd. It is a scene in nature where the lead caribou is the protector of the herd. He is in front, and as the caribou migrate, he periodically stops, looks over his shoulder to see if the others are safe, and continues to walk again." According to Rob, women's names refer to good and beautiful things in nature, like flowers and seasons.

Rob's description of his name, "Caribou Standing," illustrates the importance placed on the Cree composite self – the self-in-nature (the caribou), the self-in-the-collectivity (the herd), and the individual-in-the-self (Rob), and how all knowledge is associated to one individual. Rob stressed that there can be no leader of a herd without the herd, but it is noteworthy that he identifies himself as looking back at the herd and not ahead into the "unknown," as Western representations of leaders sometimes suggest. In relation to the Cree composite self, if the self is not well grounded in the collectivity, the whole self becomes unstable. Rob's name (like many Cree names) also exemplifies the interplay between speech acts – the act of speaking – and image acts – the use of visual metaphors – and how they function together to provide the listener with a comprehensive perception of the event. Images are more of a presentation than a re-presentation (Bakewell 1998, 22). In other words, the name "Caribou Standing" does not simply relate to the caribou or representative of the caribou but also to an illustration of a specific behaviour or role of the caribou as the protector of the herd. Both systems of communication, that is, both speech acts and image acts, coexist and are co-dependent in Cree narrative discourse. This example also shows how Cree names possess a mythopoetic quality, carrying what Meletinsky would refer to as "a mythological inheritance" (1998, xix).

As Sapir noted, "single Algonquian words are like tiny imagist poems" (1921, 228), which also applies to Cree narrative discourse. For example, in a Cree folktale I have often heard, entitled "Why the muskrat's tail looks the way it does," there are several words that, once translated, become a complete and almost exact description. The word *miyuuskamiyik* relates to the time during spring when the ice begins to break up in the water, when one may still walk on the ice if one is very careful. This is a manifestation of how some words are used to create concise images to ensure the message is conveyed as precisely as possible. It also demonstrates how the stories expressed are iconic. In Cree narration, the significance is placed not only on the narrative itself but also on the individuals, animals, and events described.

Narratives are seen as versions of reality and partial representations of the world as the individual knows it.[12] Ochs and Capps' (1996) definition of narratives as verbalized, visualized, and/or embodied framings of a sequence of actual or possible life events is relevant to Cree narrative discourse. Cree narratives often integrate two or more communicative modes, such as visual representation, gesture, facial expression, and physical activity, that can be combined with talk, song, or writing to convey a tale. What are considered as meaningful events worth communicating are often conveyed to others in a storytelling fashion rather than explained in the form of simple facts.

Cree elders often speak to me as well as to others through visual metaphors both to avoid imposing a view of the world on those who listen to them and to attempt to personalize mythologic thought. Moreover, verbal messages are validated by accumulated life experiences, which are largely non-verbal (Darnell 1988). For instance, when I was in the bush with a Cree friend of mine, I asked if he was going to set snares for rabbits. This question triggered a descriptive narrative rather than a direct response to my question. He said he was six years old and it was a cold autumn day when he followed his father into the bush, listening closely to the sounds they were making as their feet hit the ground. He had left his mother in the wigwam cleaning and smoking fish and taking care of his younger siblings. His father stopped in his path, took a deep breath, and told him that before you go hunting or setting snares, you go into the bush and ask the animals if they are ready to be hunted. He described the area in the bush in which this conversation took place, the scented pine trees, the sun coming through the trees, the smell of winter approaching. It seemed like he was trying to recreate the location of this important memory. The preceding week he had asked a rabbit if he was ready and it answered that it was not. Thus, he was just going into the bush to pick berries.

The images used in Sid's narrative were vivid and emotionally charged. When I wondered about the communication he had with a rabbit, he said that what he actually spoke to was the spirit of the rabbit. Interestingly, this narrative indicates how Cree people often embrace animals rather than exclude them, as described above, and that the hunting events are experienced and described as ongoing instances of social interaction (Brightman 1993, 2). Moreover, in this story, we see how the self is inseparable from the narrative, which is characteristic of narrative constructions (Kerby 1991). Sid's notion of self is given content and embodied by his individual experience. In narrative constructions such as Sid's, self-understanding is dependent on the coherence and continuity of one's personal narrative (Kerby 1991, 6). As exemplified in Cree narration, narratives are fundamental to one's conception of the world and one's sense of place within it. In regards to Cree narration, Brightman (1993, 57) remarks that the narratives and the persons and events they describe are alternately signs of one another, which shows how they are all metonymically linked. In other words, in Cree narration, we see how different levels of experience remain contiguous.

METONYMY AND METAPHOR

Metonymy and metaphor are characteristic elements of Cree narrative discourse. Metonymy involves taking one trait of an entity to

Figure 4.6 Tom's rabbit & lynx

represent the entity as a whole, whereas metaphor contains an implied comparison focusing on the similarity of attributes between two entities. Metonymic associations highlight one aspect of an entity by decomposing the totality of the object and singling out one of its attributes (Fernandez 1991). According to Fernandez (1991, 195), metonymy is highly individualized, and it is assembled and disassembled according to particular experience and circumstance. Oftentimes the imagery of my art therapy patient Tom involved a move from a part to a whole – the part relating to an element in his artwork that symbolized his self as a whole. An example of this process can be found in figure 4.6, where Tom drew a rabbit and a lynx and emphasized an X-ray view of both animals.[13] There is a sense of the inside and the outside of each animal figure, and both dimensions have been combined into one entity. Interestingly, Tom's artwork, as seen in this drawing, illustrates features commonly found in Algonquian artwork as described by Warner (1978). What is evident in Tom's work is a pronounced emphasis on line and form with an absence of background and an emphasis on X-ray vision, or the drawing of internal organs. Warner (1978, 76) notes that for Algonquian people, as hunter-gatherers, "the concept of showing both internal and external aspects of a figure in a painting seems to be natural enough" (1978, 76).

Tom's interpretation of this drawing (figure 4.6) was that it represented his need to go within to try to sort the fragments of his self, the chaos within. He had created this drawing while he was grieving the death of his father and dealing with his mother's hospitalization and diagnosis of cancer. For the first time in his life he felt alone and

Figure 4.7 Tom's bush cabin

misunderstood by everyone around him, and he was living in the community, a foreign place, away from home, the bush. Tom's house in the community was used as a safe haven for the alcoholics in the area. As a result, in order to feel accepted by his peers, Tom had begun drinking and abusing alcohol, which led to aggression toward others and vandalistic acts in the community. At the point when he made this drawing he was waiting for placement in a residential treatment centre in Montreal – another foreign place – for treatment for his alcoholism and for him to attend sign-language school. Figure 4.6 depicted a transition period from a focus on the external in previous drawings (figure 4.7) to an emphasis on the internal. For Tom, going within was less anxiety-provoking than was the external chaos surrounding him, and so he would use his drawing journal that I had given him as his sanctuary. He felt that he needed to address his inner insecurity and feelings of despair primarily caused by the loss of his father and from having been placed into foreign surroundings.

Tom often expressed his connection to the animal world in his artwork. A characteristic of Cree reality in general and Tom's in particular is that the fundamental basis for self-understanding is the metaphoric analogy between the human and animal domains. In

Tom's imagery, he would use animals to draw elaborate pictures of his self. Human categories and animal categories are metonymically linked, yet metaphor is used to reveal the potential relationship between two things rather than a figurative relationship. Used as models for understanding the world, metaphors are pervasive both in thought and in action (Lakoff and Johnson 1980). The Cree disposition, as seen in Tom's case, appears to include the assumption that connections among people, animals, and other entities exist, both in the physical and metaphysical dimensions (Scott 1996; Ingold 1996). As Ingold argues in terms of the metaphoric associations made between humans and animals, "the force of the metaphor is to reveal the underlying ontological equivalence of human and non-human components of the environment as agencies of nurturance" (1996, 134). Like Scott (1996, 72), I have noticed among my Cree informants that they tend to explore the nature of the possible connections between human and non-human entities, whereas the Western conventional attitude is to assume fundamental differences.

SYNAESTHASIA

One of my Cree informants once told me how she learned the Cree syllabics[14] as a child. Her parents would encourage her to look for the phonetic symbols in the trees and bushes. They believed that if she saw the symbols visually she would better integrate Cree syllabics. This form of pattern recognition reflects a dimension of an interdependence of sensory realms, in this case a cross-modal shift between vision and sound, which may be considered a synaesthetic element. It also demonstrates, again the interplay between speech acts and image acts. Synaesthasia is a process whereby a sensation produced in one modality induces the application of another sensory modality (Dann 1998, 5), such as in the example above, where a phonetic sound induces the visualization of an image.[15] Synaesthasia is defined as "a phenomenon of meaning" where "sensation develops to perception" (Wheeler and Cutsforth 1922, 220). In our description of Cree reality, a characteristic trait that appears similar to the concept of synaesthasia is its sensible qualities, whereby the knowledge system is adapted to perception and imagination and it approaches the physical world in concrete terms.[16] Moreover, the shifting from one sense to another is entirely consonant with mythopoesis and the multidimensional embodiment of the collectivity in the self and nature in the self already described.

Lakoff's 1987 notion of "image schemas" is also relevant here in terms of the synaesthetic elements of Cree perception and how objects are classified on the basis of shared shape or movement. Image schemas are defined as "schema transformations" that are visual or kinesthetic in nature, and they are "direct reflections of our experiences" (Lakoff 1987, 443). Lakoff describes the process of categorization as being dependent on "experiential aspects of human psychology," including "gestalt perception, mental imagery, motor activities, social function, and memory" (37). This description parallels the Cree process, which is defined by Preston as a "personalized mode of perception [that] yields a more event-specific categorization of the environment," where the environment is not separated from the social and mental contexts (1975, 182). As both Fulford (1998, 2000a) and I have noticed, many Cree individuals demonstrate the capacity to "read the world on the basis of fundamental iconic forms" (Fulford 2000a, 3), and the function of Cree language and synaesthetic associations is based on the need to express meaningful experience.

Synaesthasia is not presented as a form of expanded consciousness, nor is it linked to a transcendental set of meanings (Dann 1998). Rather, the process of synaesthasia allows one to attach meaning to the transcendental by making it tangible through sensations and images. Synaesthasia was often considered as being a process that involved emotions and that interfered with logical thought (Dann 1998). Howes (1991, 6) states that in Western society, we are used to our senses being dissociated from each other. I have noticed in my Cree patients and informants more of an integration of senses rather than dissociation. As described in the example above with the Cree syllabics, they appear to be manifesting a visual-type synaesthasia, where a phonetic sound might evoke a visual image or a visual stimulus might evoke a sound, taste, or tactile sensation.

As Luria described in *The Mind of a Mnemonist*, (1968) his synaesthete subject would convert senseless words into intelligible images. Similarly, when Tom arrived in Montreal for residential treatment, he attempted to make some sense of what he was experiencing by creating visual images. He drew a baseball and two bats crossed over after seeing the word "baseball" and a game and finding them strange (figure 4.8). He felt that by drawing the baseball bats and ball he would better understand something that was foreign to him. It appeared that he was trying to attach some meaning to an experience that was culturally meaningless. Tom's experience demonstrates how

Figure 4.8 Tom's baseball drawing

cross-modal shifts allow an individual to frame new words, melodies, and other auditory stimuli into what they perceive to be a familiar experience, as described by Wheeler and Cutsforth (1922, 368). On another occasion, Tom saw the words "Rocky Mountains" and, before seeing an actual picture of the Rockies, he created a painting (figure 4.9) and then a series of paintings depicting these mountains. Tom also responded extremely well to sign language probably because it combined the visual and tactile modalities, thus creating an interplay of the senses.

I found interesting correlations between Wheeler's 1920 study of a blind synaesthete and my patient Tom. Both individuals experienced colour imagery in response to tastes, odours, and tactile sensations. For instance, in one of our first sessions, Tom described the odour and taste of a beaver as gray. When asked if he would like to create it in art therapy, he chose the gray clay and made a beaver (figure 4.10). For Tom this piece captures the taste, odour, colour, and image of his

Figure 4.9 Tom's Rocky Mountains

sensory experience of a beaver. As a result, he derived satisfaction from this piece especially because it encapsulated both the thought and feeling of his own experiential knowledge of the beaver. Tom said that he remembered his first taste and smell of beaver he had as a child and gray was the colour that best described his experience, which was initially unpleasant until, with time he became accustomed to the taste and smell. This example demonstrates cross-sensory equivalences, indicating an interdependence not only of the sensory realms but also of thought and feeling (Dann 1998). It also exemplifies how Tom shifted from one embodied dimension (sight) to another (taste) in his statement that "the beaver looks and tastes gray." As in the animal encounters described in the preceding section, the experience of making the intangible visible resembles an element of the synaesthasia phenomenon.

Tom also experienced colour imagery in his dreams, whereby forms and figures were identified by their colour. He would often dream of the day he was born and all he sees through a log cabin is a ray of yellow light. He depicted this dream in a pencil drawing (figure 4.11) and then in a painting (figure 4.12). The colours, images,

Figure 4.10 Tom's clay beaver

Figure 4.11 Tom's dream (drawing)

Figure 4.12 Tom's dream (painting)

tastes, odours, and tactile sensations Tom described always involved several sensorial dimensions, often in unexpected combinations. He would not describe one dimension in isolation but always in association with other dimensions. He would not derive the part from the whole but rather he would focus on the part within the whole, which is consistent with the metonymic quality of the synaesthasia phenomenon. In other words, synaesthasia is consistent with Cree mythopoesis because it involves shifts, that is, shifting from one embodied dimension to another.[17] As in mythopoetic thought, the multiple dimensions involved in synaesthasia allow for multiple meanings.

5

Ritualizing Space through Art Therapy

Common among many of my Cree patients is how art therapy becomes a ritualized space where their mythopoetic reality set is encouraged, which in turn helps them gain greater insight. I have remained faithful to my training by providing and structuring a space defined by the rules of formation of art therapy. I negotiate the space with my patients, deciding when to meet and for how long, what materials to use, what to create, and what to talk about. This space is then given meaning by my patients. The semiotic void has already transformed this space into a ritual field, in which the paucity of elements augments the semiotic power of those few elements that are present.

SPACE TO PLACE

Space is a construct created by humans, and it is constructed differently by different people and given meaningful configurations in different ways. Hallowell (1955) states that the perception of space both requires the participation of several sense modalities and involves self-identification – in other words, the self is the reference point in perceiving space. As Hallowell writes, "the individual must not only be aware of himself but of his own position in some *spatial schema*" (1995, 185; emphasis in original). We immerse ourselves in the space and we also modify its influence (Casey 1996). As Moore asserts, "space may be understood as neither the reflection of cultural codes and meanings, nor the reflection of practical activities and functional requirements; it must be understood as the product of both" (1986, 191). Lefebvre also writes on the production of space, noting that space is not a neutral form or container but rather a set of culturally constructed relations between things within the space. Space is defined as a medium, a milieu, an intermediary, and "its role is less and less neutral, more and more active, both as instrument and as goal, as means and as end" (1991, 411).

The meanings we attach to a given space are not necessarily inherent in that space. The actions of the individuals are informed by the conceptual schemes that organize space but the actual meaning given to the space is dependent on the meanings attached to the nature of the activity concerned (Moore 1986). Applying Bourdieu's "theory of practice," Moore adds that "meaning is invoked through practice and is thus context-dependent" (78). Bourdieu (1977, 2) maintains that the meanings are not just the products of action but also function as principles that inform action. Consequently, both the "actions" and the space where the actions take place are given particular meanings by the individuals involved.

When the amorphous space is given meaning by an individual, it becomes an articulated place (Tuan 1977), that is, one defined by the actual experience (or activity) occurring in the place and the meaning attached to the experience. Space is abstract and undifferentiated and place is concrete, particular, and emotion-laden (Ryden 1993, 37). Ryden (1993) elaborates that although space contains place, place is more than an object of thought. Place is a "center of meaning constructed by experience" (Tuan 1975, 152). Casey argues that the experience of space is not a secondary grid overlaid on the presumed primacy of space; "Rather ... place is the most fundamental form of embodied experience – the site of a powerful fusion of self, space, and time" (1996, 9). My Cree informant's description of Cree land, *iyiyuu estchee*, highlights how the sense of place captures the fusion of self, space, and time. According to Ella, "*iyiyuu estchee* is not just a geographical location, but a state of mind." She explained to me that she thinks *with* the landscape and not just *about* it. Ella added that the animals, the plants, the berries, the sunset and sunrise are as much a part of her as her mother, her ancestors, and her self. Ella's description concords with Jackson's observation of the Warlpiri's perception of landscape when he noted that "the human body and the body of the land share a common language. Person and place coalesce. Whatever happens to the one, happens to the other" (1995, 125). Thus, there appears to be a metaphoric condensation of the notions of place and self.

Another example of the experiential value placed on the sense of place is when Sid brought me to a hydro-electric dam and pointed out to me where he was born and raised. "We had our wigwam right there where all the rocks and water is now. I could just picture it exactly the way it was then and I could see my parents, my brothers and sisters and myself playing in that whole area surrounded by pine trees. Now there's nothing left because it was flooded." This "remembered place" has served both as a memoryscape, in which the past is anchored to space and becomes "place," and as a symbolic anchor of a sense of self for Sid and other Cree people, whose sense of self has been partially deterritorialized.[1] There is a sense of a bounded locality characterized by memories of past events, and geographic space is often used as a metaphor for self-identity (Nuttall 1992; Lanoue 2000). As demonstrated in Sid's narrative, when actual places become blurred and indeterminate, ideas of culturally and ethnically distinct places may become even more salient (Gupta and Ferguson 1992), and become subject to metonymization. Although Sid's important "place" has been drastically modified, it remains a point of security and stability in an uncertain world, providing a firm anchor in a known and valued past. Sid's narrative shows how a particular place in the landscape is imbued with meaning, given form, perpetuated, and shared. Through his memoryscape, Sid gains a sense of place, which is best described as "a way of imaginatively engaging with one's surroundings and finding them significant, a personal and cultural appropriation of the world" (Tilley 1999, 182). For Sid and many other Cree people I have met, these tangibly marked places constitute a link to their past when there existed a secure definition of what it meant to be Cree, when there was a core set of values that helped situate individuals in a social space.

Casey claims that places constitute "things, experiences, histories, languages and thoughts" (1996, 18), which implicitly relates to the fundamental quality of the continuity of meaning. Sid's sense of place as described in the above narrative can thus be seen as having been transmitted intergenerationally. In a similar vein, Cruikshank (1990) shows how three elderly women from the Yukon model and interpret their own experiences in the contexts of geography and of the exploits of their ancestors. As among many Native Americans, place names are often related to their sense of being and are seen as cultural artifacts; they serve as "touchstones in autobiographical narratives" (Thornton 1997, 220). Among the Cree individuals I work with, the sense of place they experience in a given landscape and the continuity of meaning conveyed through their narratives are instrumental to the construction of individual experience. It is precisely this sense, I argue, that is important in the art therapy milieu, which, I have pointed out, is partly ritualized by using the same place from session to session.

THE ART THERAPY MILIEU

Applying Lefebvre's framework on the production of social space, the art therapy milieu can be viewed as constituting three interrelated dimensions: (1) physical space; (2) mental space; and (3) social space. In the art therapy physical space, there are explicit boundaries. It is a limited space because of its internal structure to create art. With a variety of accessible art materials, the physical space can be defined by its "practico-sensory activity" in relation to the art-making involved (Lefebvre 1991, 27). A therapeutic environment that is both physically and psychologically safe is created and maintained (e.g. privacy and confidentiality are ensured). The development of a sense of trust and familiarity leads to the creation of an environment to create art and to engage in self-reflection. Thus, the physical space, or what I like to refer to as the external landscape, eventually is conducive to the internal landscape or mental space (Lefebvre 1991).

Lefebvre's (1991, 27) description of mental space as being occupied by sensory phenomena, such as products of the imagination, applies to the art therapy mental space. Art therapy depends on art as its chief therapeutic agent. "Its healing potentialities depend on the psychological processes that are activated in creative work" (Kramer 1971, 25). Kramer claims that "art and the creative process involve a complex comprehension both of the physical handling of art materials in order to form them so that they serve as symbolic equivalents for human experience and the psychic processes that motivate creative work" (1979, xxvii). I will show in a subsequent section how ritualization is also a significant therapeutic agent.

Art therapy can be viewed as possessing two types of discourse, both occupying a particular mental space: one relates to the art-making (i.e. the process of giving form to feeling [Langer 1953, 1962; Kramer 1979]) and the other relates to talking about the art or the interpretive dialogue. In both interdependent forms, art therapists employ certain techniques that draw the patient into a specific discourse that defines and delimits the patient's narratives of self. These features appear to constitute similar elements of Foucault's 1971 notion of discursive practice in that the patient is subject to the discourse as his or her narratives are shaped in some ways by the art therapy discourse. The art therapy "discursive practice" helps establish the boundaries of the art therapy space, which are to create art and then to describe the experience or process and/or the product. The therapist's interventions (e.g. "tell me about your drawing") can be seen as a "technique of the self" as defined by Foucault (1979) because they place the patient in a self-reflective stance and form the patient's understanding of his/her distress as a problem of the self. The therapist's interventions also aim to induce the patient to focus on the vicissitudes of her subjective experience and go beyond the narrative to find the essence. The "rules" that constitute the art therapy discourse usually involve the creation of spontaneous expression based on whatever the patient is feeling at the moment. The art-making may occur without any verbalized intention on the patient's behalf and without any suggestion made by the art therapist. At other times, I may ask the patient to complete specific art therapy diagnostic procedures, where the patient is given specific instructions (figures 5.1–5.4).[2] My Cree patients have inserted themselves into the art therapy discourse, following its "rules" and sometimes modifying them and, in turn, producing a new discourse and a new space – one that is ritualized.

The art therapeutic milieu is not a neutral environment. There is a clear purpose – a dialogic encounter that promotes an analytic stance of self-reflection, which, like other therapies, also constitutes the art therapy mental space. The reflexivity involved in the therapeutic discourse is a type of autobiographic activity. Akin to Ricoeur's 1970 theory on self-reflection, in order for the therapy to be effective, the individuals must see themselves in "the mirror … of the objects, acts, works and signs which the self produces and wherein the self is disclosed. [Self-] Reflection is thus the effort to recapture the subject or self in the 'mirror' of the objects" (cited in Moore 1990, 87).[3] Often, the artwork created acts as a mirror, which plays a significant role in an individual's gradual development of self-awareness.[4] My view of the role of art-making concords with definitions from both Langer and Gusdorf. Langer defines "the primary function of art" as objectifying feeling "so that we can contemplate and understand it. It is the formulation of so-called 'inward experience,' the 'inner life.' That is impossible to achieve by discursive thought, because its forms are

Figure 5.1 UPAP no. 1: Free drawing

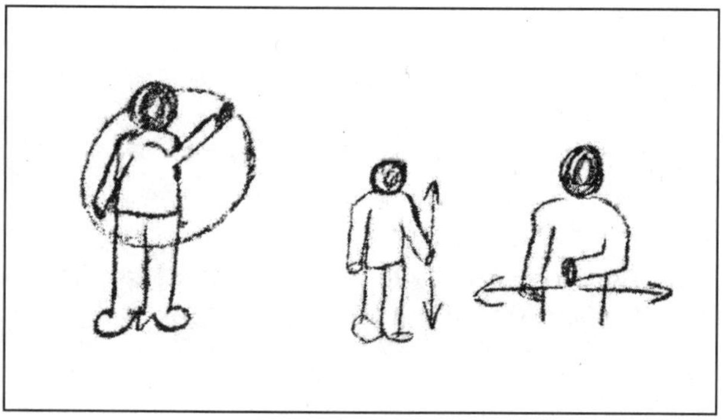

Figure 5.2 UPAP no. 2: Kinesthetic drawing

incommensurable with the forms of language" (1962, 60). As Gusdorf claims, during the self-reflexive quest for personal meanings, the individual "distinguishes that which is without from his own within, he sees himself as another among others; he is situated in social space, at the heart of which he will become capable of reshaping his own reality" (1980, 32)[5]. In this self-reflexive quest, the goal is to reassemble the scattered elements of one's individual life and regroup them into a comprehensive sketch.

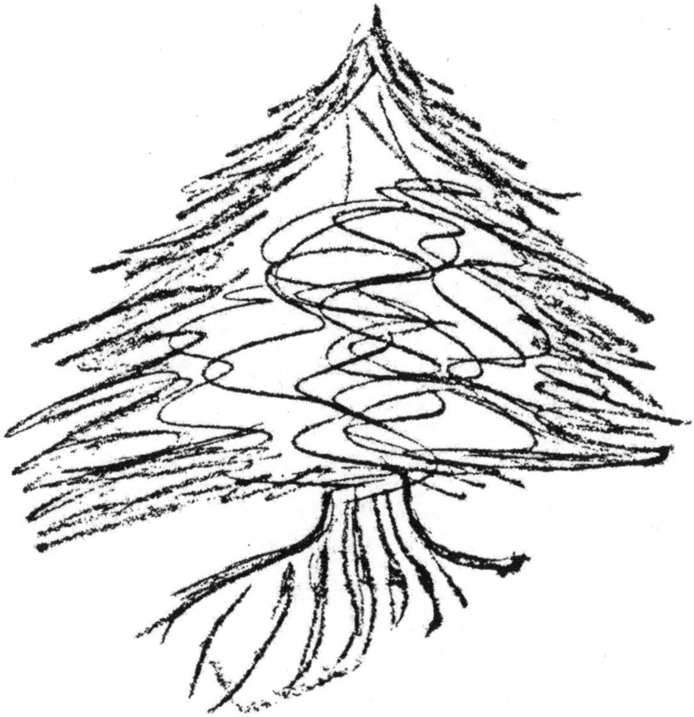

Figure 5.3 UPAP no. 3: Scribble

In art therapy, both the creation of the image and the creation of the dialogue (in the form of narratives) about the image(s) created are reflexive in nature. Although the narrative discourse in art therapy may also be found in verbal psychotherapy, the "dialogue" between the artist-patient and his/her creation has no exact parallel in talk therapy (Kramer 1979, 140). In art therapy, the artwork and the narratives provide a concrete experience of personal reflection, and both establish a context for an epiphany, or a moment of heightened self-awareness, which may or may not be facilitated by the therapist. Although the process of creating art is in itself therapeutic for many of my patients, significant meaning is created during the moments of epiphany, and once the clinical space transforms into a lived-in place through the agent of making and talking about the artwork, the space becomes ritualized. As Rubin also claims, the "potency" of art therapy is due to the combination of "a powerful, deeply involving

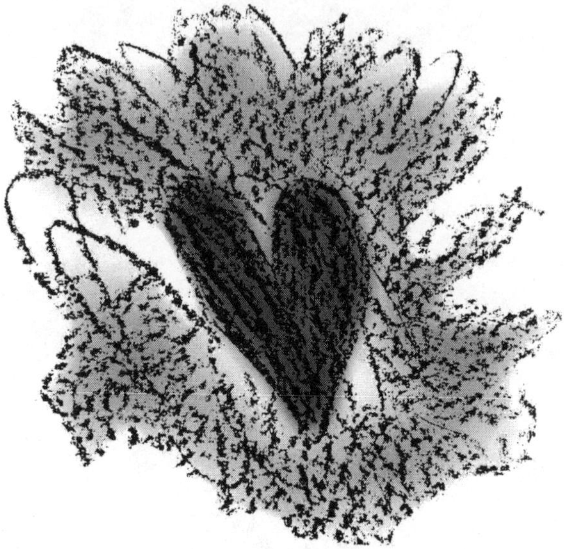

Figure 5.4 UPAP no. 4: Scribble

experience with a distancing, organizing perspective. Through both vision and words, the looking at, considering, capturing, and comprehending of the experience become possiblea true 'in-sight' ('seeing in')"(1984, 139–40). The therapy becomes meaningful when such moments of insight lead to a reassembling of the elements of the individual's inner world.

The art therapy milieu also becomes a social space, due to the therapeutic relationship established, which is based on trust. According to Lefebvre (1991, 83), the social space is a social product that incorporates actions; in relation to art therapy, the interpersonal interactions between therapist and patient, whether in regards to the art process or not, characterize this particular social space. In my interactive and dialogically conceived therapeutic encounter, I am recognizing the reciprocal influence between myself and the patient. This approach functions to structure my mode of listening and my interventions, which in turn play a role in shaping the patient's experience and mode of response.[6] In art therapy, all three spaces – the physical, mental, and social – are interrelated, and they are intimately bound up with function and structure. It is also possible that these multiple dimensions make this therapy appealing because it concords with the creation of multiple selves-within-the-self. Because the multiple dimensions allow for the possibility of multiple meanings, the limited number of elements within the space becomes ritualized. The art therapy space becomes a marked place for many of my Cree patients, and one with semiotic potential. My Cree patients temporarily "dwell" within what becomes a semantically filled art therapy space.

RITUAL SPACE

According to Victor Turner, a ritual is a sequence of activities involving gestures, words, and objects performed in a sequestered place (1973, 1100). Essentially, a ritual is transformative (V. Turner 1979), and it is a performance, an enactment, and not just primarily rules or rubrics (V. Turner 1981, 160). This definition of ritual can easily be applied to psychotherapy in general and art therapy in particular because both are healing rituals with their own symbols. Bell (1997, 102) claims that psychoanalysis and ritual theory possess many parallels, in that "the process of human individuation that leads to the achievement of a mature sense of self" is promoted in both.[7] Both ritual and psychoanalytic experiences effect transition in the psychological and social spheres, and both usually occur in a sequestered place. Art therapy is an experience that occurs on the peripheries of everyday life. By promoting self-reflection, the art therapy process may invoke transition, such as a broadened self-awareness and a stronger sense of inner security.

My Cree patients undertake to change the initially semantically void art therapy space into an articulated space. Its constant elements, such as the same therapist, same materials, same room, and the ongoing engagement, provide a sense of continuity and contribute to the ritualization of the art therapy experience and of its signs. By ritualization, I mean that art therapy becomes a way of acting that is distinct from other activities in the individual's life. Bell's theory on ritualization is relevant here. She defines ritualization as a strategic way of acting that creates and privileges a qualitative distinction between the "sacred" and the "profane" (1992, 74). The art therapy space has structure and consistency, which become highly significant in the process of ritualization, and its formality enhances its communicative efficacy. According to both Bell (1992, 92) and Rappaport (1999, 51), rituals are intensive forms of communication by virtue of their repetition and sacredness.

The art therapy ritual is more than a matter of routine; it is granted a privileged distinction because it occurs in a delineated and structured space to which access is restricted. I agree with Rappaport's declaration that "ritual is not simply an alternative way to express any manner of thing, but that certain meanings and effects can best, or even *only* be expressed or achieved in ritual" (1999, 30). I believe that the art therapy ritual is a unique structure differentiating itself from other "spaces." Although none of its elements, such as performance, formality and repetitiveness, belong to it alone, the relation among them is unique to the art therapy ritual space.

Strategies for differentiating itself from other ways of acting are intrinsic to ritualization (Bell 1992). Art therapy can be seen as a "way of acting" that makes the following distinctions: (a) a special time for the occurrence of the art therapy session with the art therapy "specialist"; (b) the internal orchestration of the art-making process (i.e. the patient may either choose the type of art activity, or suggestions are made by the therapist, or specific art materials are provided for particular art therapy assessments); (c) the specific codes of communication or what Rappaport (1999, 151) defines as ritualized gestures and words are used (i.e. verbal and gestural combinations, such as the therapist placing the artwork at some distance for the patient to describe his/her piece and experience). The ritual acts and objects in the art therapy space, such as the art materials and the artwork created, have special communicational qualities. All these features of the ritual form add something to the substance or the symbolic meaning of the art therapy ritual space.

A double ritualization occurs within art therapy. The first involves my role in creating the art therapy space: I structure the situation by offering the patient a limited number of art materials and a limited amount of time in the art therapy milieu. The space becomes defined by such limitations and the structure defines what people can do or think. It becomes a space with a purpose, a symbolic space grounded in experience.

The second dimension of the ritualization process is the patient's role and how he/she attaches meaning to the structured space. This is illustrated in Luke's drawings of the two of us in art therapy (figures 5.5 and 5.6). It was only when Luke felt accepted and understood by me that he was ready to draw himself. In figure 5.5, he drew me looking at and listening to him, and in figure 5.6, he drew the two of us hugging each other. Both drawings also relate to the safe and nurturing context Luke experienced, and thus symbolize his sense of containment while in art therapy.

Figure 5.5 Luke's drawing of the two of us

Figure 5.6 Luke: The bush and art therapy

Luke, like many of my patients, attached meaning to the creative art process, to the artwork he produced (from which he derived a sense of pride), and to our therapeutic relationship. The interactive dialogue, or "dialogic exchange" (Schafer 1981), between the patient and myself, which becomes both a medium and product of this interaction, is instrumental in attributing meaning to the ritual space.[8] The dialogic exchange inspires the patient to engage in a self-reflexive narrative, which allows him/her to establish some distance among the various components of the self (individual self, self-in-the-collective, self-in-nature). The interaction between the therapist and the patient as narrator serves to construct the meaning of the personal narratives and the meaning attached to the therapeutic milieu. I also employ a ritualistic form of therapeutic rhetoric to empower the patient, which is an element in most psychotherapeutic approaches (Frank and Frank 1991). This ritualized therapeutic rhetoric involves listening to my patients with interest, acknowledging what they say, and validating what they create. My therapeutic interventions rely on the patient's narratives of self. Both my faith and the patient's faith in the intervention I provide, along with the patient's trust in me, play a significant role in the ritualization of art therapy.

In my interpretation of art therapy as a ritual space, Victor Turner's theoretical framework on the ritual process has assisted me into organizing my observations both as a clinician and ethnographer. I have found both his work in *The Ritual Process* (1969) and Arnold van Gennep's theory of ritual as a separate social space relevant. In *The Rites of Passage* (1909), van Gennep (1909, 13) demonstrates that many types of rituals have three distinguishable stages of varying duration among various cultures: (1) separation (preliminal) stage involves the detachment of the individual from an earlier fixed point in a set of cultural conditions; (2) margin or limen (liminal) stage is ambiguous and it is the "betwixt and between" stage where the transition usually occurs; and (3) reaggregation (postliminal) involves the consummation of the passage characterized by stability. Van Gennep argued that rituals are often performed when individuals need to experience a change of state or status as defined by their cultural group. The *rites de passage* are not necessarily confined to culturally defined life-crises but may accompany any change from one state to another (V. Turner 1979). In this case, I am not arguing that the liminality of the therapy space is in itself transformative, but that the distancing of the components of the self temporarily places each in a separate, unique, and, for the Crees, highly artificial (and therefore liminal) space.

Although there are ritual elements in art therapy, the art therapy experience may not be a "sacred ritual" with an inherently spiritual purpose. However, by its nature it could be recognized as what Turner refers to as a "liminoidal" event, characterized by marginality, creativity, reformation, and transition (1974, 15). On the other hand, art therapy is hardly a spectacle, as are many liminoidal events. So perhaps it is a "sacred" ritual in a "secular" world.[9] The goals of transformation and empowerment in art therapy are parallel to the goals of re-establishing harmony in the social dramas as expounded by Turner (1967, 1969, 1981). Thus, the art therapy ritual may provide (temporary) resolution to the individual's "dramas," as it helps my patients re-establish personal harmony through the processes of self-reflection, individuation, and reintegration of the components of the self.[10]

By validating their creations within the limited ritual space, I enrich the semiotic power of the interpretive signs my patients attribute to their work. These interpretive signs have properties of what Turner (1967, 28; 1965) calls condensation and multivocality in his discussion on dominant ritual symbols.[11] Condensation refers to many things represented in a single formation, which is saturated with emotion. Multivocality suggests the referential openness and ambiguity of a symbol, and it promotes the possibility of transforming an individual's understanding of social conventions and cultural beliefs through associations made between private symbols and public symbols (V. Turner 1965, 50; 1967). This is similar to the metonymic associations found in Cree narrative discourse. Essentially, the multivocality of ritual symbols helps interconnect individual experience with social experience. In art therapy, the artwork, as the dominant ritual symbol, possesses two poles of meaning, relating to the property of "polarization of meaning" (V. Turner 1967, 28), as well as that of multivocality and condensation. The two poles of meaning include the sensory and the ideological, where the former evokes desires and feelings and the latter relates to the values and norms of the social group: at "the sensory pole, the meaning content is closely related to the outward form of the symbol" (V. Turner 1967, 28). Tom's drawing of the caribou (figure 4.2) illustrates the properties of the dominant symbol as defined by Turner. The sensory pole in this drawing relates to Tom's animal-doctor relationship with the caribou, and the ideological pole relates to how Crees honour the caribou as a game animal that represents power. For Tom, the caribou symbol was transformed into an agent of well-being, as he received the gift of strength from the caribou during his encounter. This transformation resembles Turner's (1967) definition of a symbol's property of multivocality because it illustrates how the caribou as a Cree symbol was given personal meaning. Tom also drew a "medicine wheel" (figure 5.7), which he interpreted as representing a childhood memory of his father.[12] His father had explained the medicine wheel as combining the four races, four directions, and four seasons, and he did so by carving it out in birchbark while in the bush. Tom was told that it symbolized life. Particular to Tom's interpretation of the medicine wheel are the drumsticks he added behind the wheel, which in a sense doubled as an image of the traditional Eastern Cree drum. This related to his memory of his father playing the drum while in the bush. The five feathers he added around the wheel symbolize Tom and his siblings. When Tom drew this picture, using watercolour markers, he was in the process of developing closer relationships with his siblings: because he had lived most of his life in the bush, he rarely spent time with his siblings, who lived primarily in the community. After being relocated to the community following his father's death and his mother's illness, he began re-acquainting himself with his siblings, who in turn were quite involved in Tom's healing process. During his residential treatment, Tom was learning how to use his voice during drumming ceremonies held at the house, as he would hum while feeling the vibrations of the drum. Thus, the medicine wheel that he drew symbolized a link to his past as well as the healing process he was engaged in.

The medicine wheel has come to represent, for many Aboriginal people I have worked with, the unity and continuity of First Nations Peoples, as it is seen as a culturally universal symbol.[13] Thus, as I understand it, a dominant symbol can integrate both personal and collective representations, creating an interchange of qualities between both poles of meaning (V. Turner 1967).

The "rules" of the art therapy process frame the ritual process, but the ritual process transcends its frame, especially when the patient uses the art therapy ritual to transform him/herself, that is, to engage in some form of transition or resolution. Within the art therapy space, there are what Turner (1969, 1974) would refer to as symbolic operators or vehicles (i.e. the artwork, narratives that stem from the artwork, the relationship between patient and therapist) that can effect change on the individual occupying the space. During the therapeutic process, the patient engages in a self-discovery process that usually leads to self-transformation and the resolution of conflicting feelings and issues. The transitional period resembles a threshold, which can be defined as a liminal transition and a domain of action or thought (V. Turner 1974, 52). The period of margin or liminality is an "interstructural" phase (V. Turner 1979, 234), one that involves reflec-

Figure 5.7 Tom's medicine wheel

tion of one's thoughts and feelings.[14] In this process of reflection, the individual engages in the undoing, dissolution, and decomposition of aspects of one's self. This experience is then accompanied by "processes of growth, transformation and the reformulation of old elements in new patterns" (237). Unlike Turner, I do not believe that the "neophyte in liminality must be a *tabula rasa*, a blank slate" (1969, 103). I believe that the ritualizing aspects of the art therapy session act as a liminal phase, interrupting "normal" thinking and encouraging (if not obliging or simply allowing) individuals to rethink and reformulate old patterns. The artificial nature and limited number of elements in the art therapy ritual space metonymically set in motion a deconstruction of old patterns as "superfluous" elements of the self are shed, while remaining elements are re-semioticized and then reshuffled. I ritualize the space by providing the patients with constant elements and they ritualize it by engaging in deconstructing elements of the self and then re-incorporating them. Essentially, what heals is that they are healing themselves in a ritualized space.

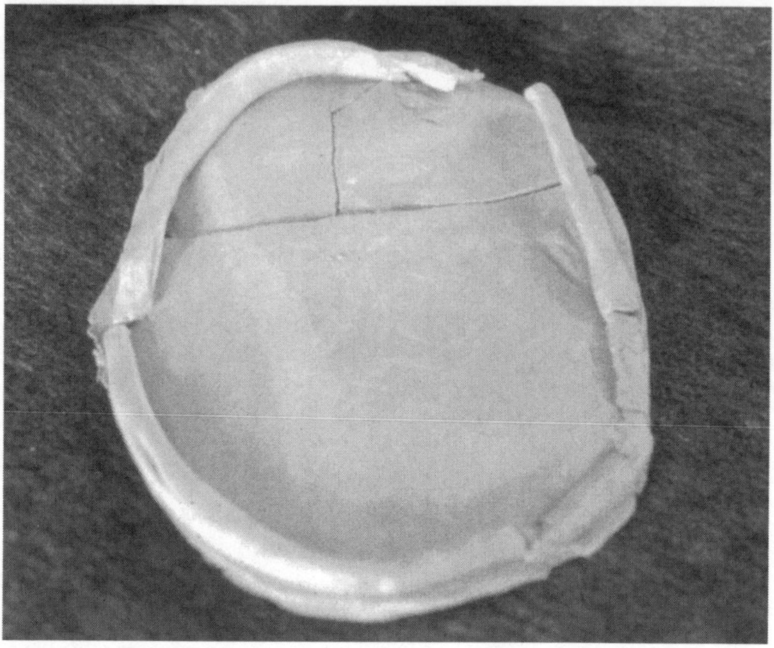

Figure 5.8 Luke's clay coin

An example of the process of undoing and decomposition is apparent in Luke's experience of drawing and then destroying his artwork and creating clay sculptures and breaking it up into pieces. This often occurred during the beginning sessions of therapy. In one session, Luke destroyed a clay sculpture by throwing all the bits of clay across the art therapy room. Pieces of clay were on the walls, ceiling, and the floor. He then gathered all the pieces together and created a large coin, as he called it (figure 5.8).

Luke was dealing with a fragmented sense of self, experiencing frustration, anger, and sadness about being away from home and his family; being hearing-impaired; not being allowed to go to the bush when at home because of his hyperactivity; and while in Montreal, being surrounded by the Euro-Canadian culture, which of course was foreign to him. This art experience also represented a perceived disintegration of all that was of value to Luke. His clay "coin" symbolized the tension between undoing and reformulating "the having been and the becoming" or between his fragmented self and his healed self. It symbolized his need to deconstruct the old and reformulate his new sense of self. Being physically detached from his family and his community forced Luke to confront his fragmented self. Once he gained an inner sense of security, facilitated by the sense of containment he experienced in the art therapy ritual space and the trust he developed with me, he was able to transform the ambiguity and ambivalence into stability and clarity and consequently into a more secure, better-integrated sense of self. Near the end of therapy, Luke's "passage was consummated" (V. Turner 1969, 1979) when he had gained an autonomous, healed self, which was recognized by his family as they brought him into the bush to experience the killing of his first goose (figure 4.5).

"Healing" for the Crees is not getting back to a norm but creating a new self by deconstructing the old, redefining the components, and building a new, multidimensional and more harmonious self. While in residential treatment in Montreal, Tom also experienced an ambiguous state of not being here nor there. While in the self-reflective state, he experimented with images of the foreign symbols surrounding him (figures 4.8 and 4.9). He would then create images that symbolized more of his internal struggle as he interpreted it (figure 5.9). Once he resolved his issues and developed a sense of inner security, Tom's transition was consummated during his reintegration into his community, which relates to the reaggregation phase of rituals. Tom's Cree community worker and I organized an art exhibition of his artwork, re-introducing him back into the community as an artist.

The development of trust and stability leads to a sense of containment in the therapeutic milieu, where emotions, dialogue, and interactions are held, whether within the artwork, the art-making process, the therapeutic relationship, or in all three. Winnicott (1949, 245), a renowned psychoanalyst whose theories I often apply in my own work as a psychotherapist, developed the notion of "the holding environment," the containment and the safe and nurturing context provided in therapy, similar to that provided by a mother for her infant. According to Winnicott (1971), this holding environment becomes a psychological transitional space, where the individual relates to the inner and outer realities by using symbols, referred to as transitional objects. The art therapy milieu often becomes a transitional space, when patients use it to engage in self-reflection and self-transformation and the artwork becomes the transitional object. Winnicott (1971, 126) also claims that within therapy a "potential space" is created, which he defines as an intermediate area that is neither inside nor outside but somewhere in

Figure 5.9 Tom's dragon

between, a space between shifting fantasy and reality realms where boundaries are not yet firmly established. Creative and spontaneous gestures are initiated in this potential space, and it is where the transitional object resides. As described by Rudnytsky (1993, xiii), Winnicott views art as a refuge where "precarious oscillations between illusion and reality" that occur in the potential space are negotiated.

Winnicott also affirms that the process of self-reflection enables the individual "to postulate the existence of the self" (1971, 64). In my case illustration of Luke, art therapy became a transitional space, a refuge, a space apart to reflect on problem areas, rectify them when he felt secure enough, and then translate his inner sense of security into his outside world to reengage himself within it. This space apart also resembles Turner's notion of liminality, where the individual needs to be separated from the daily realities of social life in order to engage in self-transformation. Bachelard's work on the poetics of space also seems relevant here in that he defines this "space apart" as a space where "the meditating being might be free to think" (1969, 231). My argument is that in regard to my Cree patients a similar process of self-reflection and sense of containment occurs in the bush; hence associations made between art therapy and the bush. The bush may also be viewed as a transitional space, as seen with Luke's killing of his first goose, with the goose head, hung in the centre of the wigwam during the ritual that follows (figure 2.2), as his transitional object, appropriated by Luke as a subjective object (i.e. one symbolizing his self-transformation in the bush).

The art therapy ritual space creates a condition of atemporality and a temporary loss of the problematic social self, which according to my Cree patients is akin to what they experience in the bush.[15] There is a withdrawal from normal modes of social action during the designated art therapy time and place, which allows a reconfiguration of signs that possibly concords with mythological meanings of a "healed" autonomous self. This is illustrated in Tina's drawing of the bush and her description of how she is separated from "the outside forces" and allowed to be herself, which was the same feeling she experienced in art therapy (figure 5.10). According to Tina, a forty-year old Cree woman, "the animals, the land and the water are part of just the way it is in the bush – simple not complicated like what is on the outside in the Whiteman world, stuff that's not Cree. In the bush, I'm allowed to be Cree and just be who I am." Many Cree people, like Tina, feel constrained in Euro-Canadian society due to norms and codes enforced upon them. The bush provides a sanctuary where they can free themselves of the troubled and ambiguous collective self.

The art therapy ritual, unlike ritual in Turner's framework, is not a social mechanism that affirms group unity. However, it does appear to evoke mythopoetic thinking and communication patterns. According to Turner (1969, 167), in the liminal phase, social relationships are simplified and myth and ritual are elaborated, which seems to relate to my Cree patients. In art therapy, there is an amplification of culturally relevant categories such as myth. As we have seen, narratives expressed in a mythic form become experiential knowledge that is are meaningful to the patient. The narrative component of art therapy attempts to express Cree values in a forum and in a style in which there are no obvious referents to lived reality, which in turn makes cultural sense. Turner refers to this as the narrative's task of "poesis" (1981, 168), that is, of remaking and re-articulating cultural sense, and this appears relevant to my Cree patients, who feel the need to make sense of their particular life experiences. Art therapy permits my Cree patients to contextualize modern problems in a mythopoetic manner. The art therapy ritual is more than just another medium where cultural values find expression in narratives and myths. The narratives and myths facilitate the patient's self-transformation by helping the patient restore balance as he/she reformulates old elements into new patterns and a more secure sense of self.

Figure 5.10 Tina's bush drawing

METONYMIC LINKS BETWEEN ART THERAPY AND THE BUSH

The bush is more that a physical landscape: it includes ways to symbolically transmit Cree cultural knowledge through rituals such as goose break and moose break, and through sharing stories and folktales. The lifeways in the bush constitute part of the "mythic world" of many of my Cree patients and informants[16]; in the bush an individual is allowed to connect and explore the component of nature in his/her composite self. The art therapy space allows the Cree patient to express elements of his/her "mythic world" and reaffirm the Cree self: many of my Cree informants and patients often say, "I am just there and I forget everything else," in relation to both their art therapy and bush experiences.[17] This illustrates how the sense of place that is experienced in both the bush and the art therapy settings is metonymically linked to the sense of self. As metonymy refers to the indirect representation of the whole by a part, I am suggesting that there is a metonymic link between "self" (the part) and "society" (the whole).

Brody refers to the "transformation in people" when they set out for the bush. He adds that "everyone feels a sense of well-being that comes only with tasks and activities which they find deeply satisfying, which they know that they know best" (1981, 253). Along the same lines, Bierhorst notes that Cree hunters "think of themselves as leaving the unclean settlement and entering the pure spiritual domain of the forest" (1994, 142) and Speck also observes that hunters are "under the thrall of the spiritual forces of the forest" (1977, 20–1). In the bush, there is a "blending of the metaphysical and the obviously pragmatic" (Brody 1981, 37). This is what patients apparently experience in art therapy as well, where they connect with their notions of self, which are metaphysical in nature, and do so mostly through the art-making process, which they consider a pragmatic activity. In both the bush and art therapy "spaces" self-reflection is promoted; other common elements include pattern and predictability, non-verbal activity, transformative dialogue where the individual becomes empowered, and mythopoetic narrative discourse.

Later in his therapy Tom often made associations between the bush and art therapy, and his drawings of a wigwam symbolized the link between the two (figures 5.11 and 5.12). Tom entitled figure 5.11 "Going Home," and figure 5.12 as his wigwam.

According to Tom, what he felt in a wigwam was the same as what he felt in art therapy – a sense of comfort and security and a special time to connect with his self.

Luke also demonstrated this type of metonymic association in his drawing of the two of us in art therapy. On the same drawing he drew a reinforced line that connected to his experience in the bush represented by a sketch (figure 5.6). Immediately afterward, Luke created a clay sculpture of a fishing boat, which he described as the boat he went fishing in with his father for the first time (figure 5.13).

The drawing and the sculpture symbolize the sense of containment he experienced in art therapy and the bush, where in both settings his new sense of self was emerging. Also, Luke was aware that his art therapy experience was helping him to eventually return to the bush – where he had not been allowed to go for most of his life due to his impulsive behaviour – as was symbolized by the double line he drew in figure 5.6 connecting the bush and art therapy.

Figure 5.11 Tom's "Going Home"

Figure 5.12 Tom's wigwam

Figure 5.13 Luke's clay boat

With several of my Cree patients, the mythic space created in the bush is somehow recreated in the ritual of art therapy. The mythic space frames the pragmatic space offered by art therapy. Tuan describes the "mythical" space as one that "surrounds the field of pragmatic activity, to which we do not consciously attend and which is yet necessary to our sense of orientation – of being securely in the world" (1977, 86). The mythic space also couples identity with the sacred, and it is pregnant with personal meaning. In both emplaced, lived experiences, there is a facilitation of being in the world.[18]

According to a Cree elder I spoke with whose son was my patient, the association between the bush and art therapy was not surprising. "It's important to see, hear and touch what's around you and what's inside." She said that in both settings all the senses play a significant role and this type of intersensory experience gives form to feeling, which is associated with the self. Along similar lines, Langer wrote on how art gives form to feeling, noting that art "formulates our conceptions of feeling and our conceptions of visual, tactual, and audible reality together. It gives us *forms of imagination* and *forms of feeling*, inseparably; that is to say, it clarifies and organizes intuition itself" (1953, 397; emphasis in original).

The experience of giving form to feeling involves a self-reflective process, which, as we have seen, occurs during the liminal phase.

The spatial-temporal quality of "I'm just there" relates to the individual not being connected with the having been or the becoming, in what Turner (1979) defines as the "betwixt and between phase." The liminal phase is characterized by simplicity, continuous reference to mystical powers, transition, sacredness, and silence (V. Turner 1969).[19] Interestingly, according to my patients and informants, their experience in the bush is also characterized by most of these properties. The features of transition, sacredness, and silence are also relevant to their art therapy experience. In both the bush and art therapy ritual spaces, "the symbol vehicles [inherent in the liminality stage] may be unimpressive, but the messages they convey are highly complex" (V. Turner 1974, 196). For instance, the messages conveyed from the artwork are self-reflective, symbolizing personal struggles and gains, a fragmented sense of self, a harmonious sense of self, etc. The symbol vehicles in the bush are the animal-human relationships that are instrumental in the metonymic construction of self (Lanoue 2000), as illustrated in chapter 4. The introspection or self-reflection process is fundamental to both ritual forms. Both my therapeutic stance in art therapy and the bush milieu essentialize the self, and the restorative notion of balance is present in both. Many of my patients and informants often relate to the introspection that occurs in the bush, whether during a vision quest or not. According to Bob: "the bush is just where I need to be. There, I feel the strong attachment to nature and my ancestors. The animals, the sunrise, the sunset – things that haven't changed through time and that is why they're so reliable in allowing me to think and feel about who I am." Emphasizing the bush de-emphasizes the collective in the composite self.

The metamessage intrinsic to the bush ritual form is simple yet rich in cosmological meaning, and it is silent, moving beyond verbal discourse. The art therapy ritual may be seen as a symbolic portrayal of myth and cosmology, and what becomes apparent in the foregoing analysis is the relationship between mythification, ritualization, and speech. The ritualization involved in both the bush and art therapy is "designed to do what it does without bringing what it is doing across the threshold of discourse or systematic thinking" (Bell 1992, 93). Although both ritual spaces involve an intensive form of communication, they are in some ways a particularly "mute" form of activity.

The non-verbal quality of art-making resembles the non-verbal exchange with animals in the bush.[20] Langer (1953) would refer to both of these rituals as non-discursive symbolic forms that express an affective experience and evoke an emotional response. The dialogic relationship with non-human persons in the bush must move beyond words. As one informant explained, "the bond between man, animal and nature exists beyond the limits of human language." An example of this is Scott's (1996, 82) description of the Cree hunter's goose songs as expressing the spiritual and aesthetic aspects of the exchange between the hunter and the goose. The songs include vivid images of the ways in which geese fall to the hunter. This illustrates how presentational symbolism or thinking visually is more accentuated than verbal thoughts. If one is capable of such communication, then, I believe, the individual may have the proclivity to extend this capacity onto human-to-human communication. That is, the individual, like many Cree people I have met, may have a more enhanced model of communication because of this capacity to move beyond words. This is apparent in my Cree patients' and informants' use of narratives and metaphoric language, and how these narratives are metonymically linked to the self and constructed to better situate their self in the world. An image by a Cree informant that is relevant to this discussion is one I have heard often and is also described by Darnell (1981, 57): "If you look at a tree and its branches you could see how social interaction works. The strong roots are provided by cultural traditions and the branches are the people, one by one bound by their relationships to each other, not by their talk."

Moreover, in the dialogic exchange with animals there is no "vertical" hierarchy, and in art therapy, many of my patients feel that the hierarchical doctor-patient relationship is non-existent. Western codes of healing implicitly legitimize explicit hierarchies (i.e. where the doctor-therapist as the authority figure is ranked above the patient, who is seen as helpless), and they promote a rhetoric of alienated individualism, which is often inadequate in dealing with most problems of Cree people. Once trust and a sense of comfort are established, my Cree patients are able to transcend the fact that I am a white Euro-Canadian, and the vertical hierarchy between Crees and Euro-Canadians is somehow not projected onto our relationship. Consequently, the dialogue that occurs in art therapy, both on the verbal and non-verbal levels, becomes more enhanced, more intense, and more effective.

In establishing trust, a significant factor is my sensitivity in regard to how the Cree people have been collectively marginalized socio-politically by Euro-Canadian mainstream society. I believe marginalization plays an underlying role in the association made between the bush lifeways and the art therapy ritual, in that both have been marginalized in Euro-Canadian society. In other words, in Euro-Canadian society, art has been marginalized because it is considered an activity for qualified specialists (artists), and this transcends into the art therapy milieu, which has been marginalized in the psychiatric arena because it is unconventional. Many of my Euro-Canadian patients are apprehensive about creating art in the therapy setting because they are "not artists" or they "can only draw stick figures," but this type of apprehension is absent with my Cree patients.[21] I am not suggesting that Euro-Canadians cannot respond to art therapy or to experiences in the bush. These can surely be symbolically rich for both Euro-Canadian and Cree patients. Nevertheless, art appears to have a different meaning for my Cree patients in that it is not seen as a separate activity for those with a special talent. In addition, the Cree experience of being marginalized collectively may also allow them to detach more readily in order to engage in the transitional, liminal phase. Turner (1974, 52) describes liminality as a form of outsiderhood and structural inferiority, implying solitude rather than society. Such involvement in the peripheries of social life may be less challenging for Crees than it is for those who are not marginalized and who are part of the mainstream society. Perhaps my understanding of being marginalized as an artist and art therapist allows me to better comprehend my Cree patients' experience, and my sensitivity facilitates their therapeutic experience and promotes a better dialogic exchange.

RELATIONSHIP BETWEEN PLACE AND BEING

My Cree patients' description of being in art therapy, "*I am just there,*" exemplifies how the concepts of place and being are intimately linked. The art therapy place is metaphorically and metonymically tied to their sense of self. Brody's description of hunter-gatherers' perception of place and its relationship to their sense of self applies to my Cree patients: "The affirmation of an existential bond between self and place is very striking among hunter-gatherers," he writes.

"The ties to a place and its resources may be more clearly affirmed than ties to history, community or even family" (2000, 320). Ingold's (1996) analysis of hunter-gatherer notion of "dwelling" is also pertinent.[22] According to Ingold, what is significant is not the construction of place but the engagement with its constituents. In hunter-gatherer ontology, one does not necessarily formulate an intentional world[23] prior to engagement in this space. Rather, there is an active and practical engagement with the constituents of the dwelt-in world. As Ingold writes, "apprehending the world is not a matter of construction but of engagement, not of building but of dwelling, not of making a view of the world but of taking a view *in* it" (121, emphasis in the original). The individual is not creating the space but actively participating in the existing space.

Dwelling in a landscape involves the incorporation of its features into a pattern of everyday activities (Ingold 1996, 144). Ingold has coined the term "interagentivity," which he uses to highlight the constitutive quality of the "dwelt-in world" of hunter-gatherers like the Crees. In other words, human beings engage intimately with one another as well as with non-human components of the environment.[24] According to my informants, they engage in dialogue with things in the environment as much as they are *with* them. Thus, Ingold argues that the hunter-gatherer perception is more interagentive than intersubjective because it includes their intimate knowledge and relations with the non-human environment. Nature is an agent and an active participant in the construction of reality, rather than a passive backdrop. The metaphorical connections drawn between landscape and behaviour form a fundamental part of the Cree notion of self. Metaphors provide the ontological basis for "dwelling" in the landscape and for reflecting on the process of interacting with it (Ingold 1996).

Many of my patients described how in the art therapy place they are allowed to think and feel through their art production. There is a dialectical process between their direct engagement in the art-making process and the thoughts and feelings expressed in the artwork. The art therapy place combines both an "action space" characterized by the art-making and a "thought/feeling space" characterized by the thoughts and feelings symbolized in the artwork. Ingold emphasizes the dynamism of the relationship between the two spaces: "action does not serve to translate pre-existent form from one domain (the mental) to another (the material); rather, form arises and is held in place *within* action: it is movement congealed" (1996, 146; my emphasis). The meanings attached to a given space are created, sustained, or manipulated through the actions executed in that space.

In the Cree dictionary, art is associated with *miyupimaatisiiun* or "being alive well." Art-making involves work that relates to life, and this suggests Crees are more sensitive to process rather than to the final result.[25] The individual engaged in art-making is working in order to feel better. Luke's drawing of the two of us in art therapy (figure 5.5) illustrates the dialectical relationship between "action space" and "thought space." Luke drew this picture at the mid-point of his therapeutic process. He initially said all he wanted to draw was what he saw, and he pointed to my arm, mid-torso area, and my head, all of which had communicative value for him because he was hearing-impaired. This was the first time Luke had drawn himself in art therapy, and it symbolized his increased sense of security with his self. He drew himself leaning with his elbows on the table and his feet grounded on the floor, suggesting how secure he felt in the art therapy space. Luke felt understood and accepted by me. He carefully wrote our names above and added the markers beside him on the table. He expressed how pleased he was with his drawing, which he simply entitled "the two of us in art therapy."

I found similarities between Basso's (1996) ethnographic inquiry on the Western Apache's notions of space and those of the Cree people I work with. Luke's experience shows how the "self-conscious experience of place is inevitably a product and expression of the self whose experience it is, and therefore, unavoidably, the nature of that experience (its intentional thrust, its substantive content, its affective tones and colorings) is shaped at every turn by the personal and social biography of the one who sustains it" (Basso 1996, 55). A sense of trust led to a social bond, and, along with the sense of continuity Luke experienced, these elements added to the meaning he attached to his sense of place in art therapy. Basso claims that notions of space are intimately linked to notions of selfhood among the Apache. Similar to Ingold's concept of interagentivity, Basso offers the term "interanimation" (55) to describe the constant mutual moulding of places and the people who dwell in them. Apparent among the Apache as well as the Cree individuals I work with is that beyond the exterior reality of place or landscape there is an interior landscape, one that belongs to the moral imagination and influences both the sense of place and the sense of self (Basso 1996).[26] Knowledge is keyed to individual lived reality, and so the launching point of the knowledge process is the individual and his or her "interior landscape."

My Cree patients' experience in the art therapy space can be described as interagentive or interanimative in that they engage intimately with the constituents of the art therapy milieu, and the artwork they create, drawing from their interior landscape, evokes metonymic connections to their self.

6

Conclusion: Art Therapy as an Interstice for the Cree Self

I began this study with the idea that I would be exploring reasons as to why my Cree patients have responded so positively to the art therapy service I provide. I have realized that art therapy with these patients becomes an interstitial space that intervenes between Cree reality and the Euro-Canadian mainstream, akin but not identical to the anthropological process by which a dialogic relationship develops between anthropologist and informant. It allows the Cree individual to focus on and try to resolve the contradictory and ambiguous tendencies in the construction of the modern Cree self. I provide my patients with the space to connect with their cultural identity, which is not necessarily recognized and validated in mainstream Euro-Canadian society. The art therapy space is more than just another "anthropological place" (Augés' 1995, 51); it is an example of a concrete and symbolic construction of space that *allows* for the expression of the vicissitudes and contradictions of social life that affect the Cree individual.

As argued here, the rhetorical structure of art therapy placed in a distinctive semantic field leads to the creation of a ritual space. It is not just about the silence or the ritualization process in art therapy, but rather the recomposed narratives of self. The epistemology of the Cree self is mythopoetic, and the art therapy rhetorical structure encourages mythopoetic shifts and substitutions among the components of self. The narrative discourse amplified in art therapy exemplifies Cree mythopoetic thought, and it is used as a tool to reconcile very distinct aspects of the Cree self that have been given ontological reality, such as the individual self, the self-in-nature, and the self-in-the-collectivity. The narratives facilitate the transition from a fragmented vision of self to a healed, composed self – an image that is experienced internally as being whole. The patients see themselves in the stories they tell of their life experiences, and so, because of this self-reflection, the narratives become the most critical aspects of their therapeutic process. Narratives are fundamental to their conception of the world and their sense of place within it, and once the narratives are listened to and validated by another in the therapeutic milieu, the self is in turn acknowledged. Consequently, the individual becomes more secure in situating his/her self in the world. Mythopoetic thought gives pattern and continuity to human perception and experience (Danesi 1993, 49), and by its repetitive character, the art therapy ritual provides a message of pattern and a sense of continuity through which the Cree individual develops a sense of security. Continuity metonymically evokes the past and facilitates the use of "traditional" elements in the negotiated identities that appear in the ritual (clinical) space.[1]

TOWARD RECOMPOSITION OF THE CREE SELF

The art therapy ritual space that my Cree patients have engaged in may be seen as a practice that involves the exploration and reflection of the Cree self, which is a marker of Cree cultural identity. This process does not necessarily relate to the survival of "tradition" or past ways of life; it is more of "a complex interplay between the continual reinvention and redefinition of the self on the one hand and, on the other, a mythological interpretation of events" (Lanoue 1995, 4). Thus, the ritualization that occurs in the art therapy space is perhaps more of a reformulation of their notions of self and their mythologic thought – a process of negotiation of the areas of ambivalence in one's life and reconciliation of distinct aspects of the Cree self.[2] Aspects of Cree ways of the past remain as active elements in the constitution of the world of many Cree individuals.[3]

Similar to the vitality found in the Quebec Cree culture, McLeod (2000, 449) shows how the Plains Cree culture is also a dynamic entity, "open-ended and multi-layered," and characterized by "narrative memory" as "an ongoing conversation with a constant play between the present, past and the future." My Cree patients and informants have shown how narratives, as part of a collective discourse, are constantly reshifting due to the dynamic character of their culture. The narratives are told in hopes of making sense of the liminal, ambiguous space that exists in Cree notions of their collective self. McLeod refers to this constant reshaping of collective discourse as "narrative irony," which is quite relevant to the Cree belief shared by many of my informants that the world can always be re-described. Similar to the multiple meanings inherent in mythopoetic thought as described in this study, McLeod adds that in Cree narrative "no interpretation can ever exhaust any narrative: there are always new ways of looking at stories, and each person who participates in the ongoing collective discourse adds layers of meanings and points to new interpretative possibilities" (450). In the art therapy ritual space, patients engage in developing a narrative link between the present and the past.

Art therapy appears as a practical way of dealing with the stress some Cree individuals experience. In times of stress, we often turn to figurative language and to the argument of images to achieve a wider and more transcendent view of things and to create a sense of wholeness.[4] Art therapy may also be seen as a form of "symbolic healing," which is described by Dow (1986) as involving the use of culturally specific symbols (in this case, Cree mythopoetic thought) that have generalizing effects on social experience and are intrinsic to a culture's model of reality. According to Dow (1986, 56), in the process of symbolic healing, the healer helps the patient particularize a cultural mythic world and manipulate healing symbols within it. In art therapy, my Cree patients create narratives by relating to their "mythic world" as a fertile source of metonyms with which new selves can be constructed and "healed."

The narrated selfhood as demonstrated in art therapy is a type of survival for my Cree patients. Also, "a narrated self founded on contextual meanings may be transitory, adapting and changing to discursive and spatial venues" (Brass 1999, 98). In relation to my Cree patients, the meanings derived from their narratives of self may be influenced by the art therapy discursive practice and symbolic space. However, I have noticed with my patients that the narrated self is less transitory and, in fact, becomes more meaningful when metonymic links are made to bush experience. As we have seen, narratives expressed in mythic form become experiential knowledge, which is retained because it is meaningful to the patient and keyed to the individual's lived reality. It becomes internalized and thus more permanent and less transitory.

My Cree patients, who have experienced collective demotivation and inconsistency in their construction of self, have turned to the symbolic, metonymic dimensions inherent in art therapy to create more adequate representations of self. As they face different and evolving conditions, the Cree individuals I have met and worked with are simply shifting to metaphoric, semantic domains that they find relevant. Essentially, my patients find rhetorical coherency in the ritualized aspects of the art therapy space.

The art therapy discourse has been reinterpreted by my Cree patients to accommodate to a Cree idiom of experience, that is, to redefine their notion of self within a mythopoetic framework. Preston (1988) would classify this process of reinterpretation as an example of syncretism. The Cree use of art therapy also exemplifies a form of medical pluralism, combining a Western approach to healing (psychotherapy) with Cree mythopoesis to deal with their fragmented sense of self. In their assemblage of different perspectives, there are processes that "communicate an understanding of how the ancestors once did things, others attempting to define the essential Cree way of life, in contrast to the ideas and technologies of outsiders. Taken together, they provide insight into the increasingly insistent call for medical pluralism" (Niezen 1997, 466). The Cree people tend to be more exclusionary, as they are guarded in their relations with Euro-Canadians (Tanner 1999) since Cree epistemology has often been "outmoded" in Euro-Canadian society by the fiction of "tradition." Nevertheless, they have incorporated art therapy, a Western innovation, into their ways of doing things because, I believe, it is a rhetorical strategy that promotes an effective forum in which to recompose the self, and because their epistemology aligns with some of the assumptions of art therapy. It allows them to return to their cultural proclivity, or what Bourdieu (1977) refers to as "habitus," which is characterized by mythologic thought.[5] Mythopoesis is a process that symbolizes an essential Cree way of thinking and art therapy is a Western-created healing practice that encourages the use of mythopoetic thought.

Cree mythopoetic discourse can be defined as a collective-type discourse because it constitutes the conditions on how people communicate and practice knowledge (Foucault 1972). It is a discourse that informs individual experience and constitutes realities by which individuals live.[6] However, I believe that we should not disregard the individual's active role in the expression and constitution of identities effected through discourse. As shown by my Cree patients and informants, the individual is an important source of meaning and thus should not be decentred in the constitution of discourse. For instance, the narratives relating to animal imagery relate to collective, "traditional" discourse. They are perhaps informed by this discourse, but each individual's unique experience of an animal-doctor relationship contributes to the constitution of the discourse. Thus, animal-doctor discourse both constitutes the realities of Cree individuals and is constituted by Cree individual narratives. Cree discourse as manifested in art therapy can be seen as a symbolically mediated and interactionally coordinated form of behaviour, which relates to Burke's (1973) theory on how rhetorical usage affects others.[7]

Because it is initially silent, art therapy does not engage some standard postulates of Western psychotherapy and it does not impose an ideologically sanctioned rhetorical structure. For instance, psychoanalysts tend to place emotional distress into a frame of meaning or rhetorical structure that assumes that negative informative influences, such as unresolved emotional conflicts stemming from childhood, are contributing factors to the malaise of people. The art therapy I provide allows the *patient* to interpret the events of their life and then situate them within frameworks of meaning that may be more culturally appropriate and sensitive to the individual's needs. Because my approach is more patient-centred, I try not to impose a rhetorical structure on them but rather encourage them to create one of their own, in hopes that they will better retain such experiential-based reality. Thus, my approach is effective with the Crees because of the value they place on individualized knowledge that is firmly rooted in lived reality. For my Cree patients, a rhetorical structure based on their personal narratives is more dynamic and real, and thus better integrated and remembered. It is this process that leads to a more healthy composite self.

MYTH, ART AND SELF-REFLECTION

It makes sense to my Cree patients to use art as an integral part of their self-reflective process because my Cree patients believe, as I do, that art is linked to the process of individuation and is directly tied to the process of spiritual self-control; this is individuation in the Cree sense, allowing for the multiple self. As Langer (1942) also claims, art provides an intermediate sphere between the physical, biological experience and the metaphysical, spiritual realms. Similarly, Lévi-Strauss defines art as lying "half-way between scientific knowledge and mythical or magical thought" (1966, 22). The process of producing an art object created in art therapy becomes a schema to organize the messages that stem from one's sense of self. According to my Cree patients and informants, this intermediate realm is also made accessible in the bush. Animals are believed to possess "two dimensions of existence, the first mundane, and the other transcendental and normally invisible" (Lanoue 2000, 2). Art therapy provides the space to express such beliefs and give tangible form to intangible experience through the art-making process. Thus, as I have shown, the metonymic links between art therapy and the bush make a lot of sense to my Cree patients, as does the metonymic association made between these ritualized spaces and the Cree sense of self because of the relationship between the process of mythification and self-expression. The sense of place experienced in both the bush and art therapy sustains identity and provides connections to a personal and collective past while offering an emotional centre. The bush has always been a place of healing and renewal, an arena of both ordinary and ritual activity, whereas art therapy has become a ritual space of self-discovery and healing.

Myths, like art, are "efforts to construct and maintain a sense of place – to create a world that resonates to human needs and desires out of neutral environment" (Tuan 1991, 687). Both myth and art can be seen as texts that are carriers of information and forms of expression that help address inconsistencies in the self. In this sense, they both have a purpose. Because my patients are dealing with contradictions in their sense of self, they turn to myths, which inherently address contradictions and function to resolve such inconsistencies. Myths are appealing because they are instrumental in transforming chaos into a special, self-referential language. The nature of metonymic code switching that defines mythologic is in fact well suited to dealing with the ambiguity of identity construction between Cree and Western thought forms. According to D.H. Turner in his analysis of Lévi-Strauss's study of myth and folklore, the contradictions myths address are derived from an already constructed and meaningful reality. He adds, "Mythical thought takes to pieces and reconstructs events which are significant within the culture – images which are already imbued with meaning" (1979, 119). The process in art therapy is similar in that it involves a rethinking, reconstructive process of elements relevant to the Cree self, which are imbued with meaning. In this rethinking process, individuals gain inner strength and security first to enhance the qualities of self that are already present and then to take what is necessary from the contradictory rhetorics of self-making to construct a more balanced, secure identity that is functional in both the Cree context and the Euro-Canadian mainstream.

CREE SELF – RELATIONAL OR INDIVIDUATED?

We have seen that the self-reflection process and the narratives of self that emerge may be influenced by the art therapy discourse. John Berry's work on Cree cognitive style (Berry 1976; Berry and Bennett 1992), specifically focusing on self/non-self segregation in relation to the individual's processing of information and the degree to which it is affected by the contextual field, is relevant here. My patients have often demonstrated how they think with the art therapy space, in that they use the elements of the space and the art therapy rhetoric to engage in self-reflection. This type of processing would be categorized as field dependent because the process is dependent on and influenced by the contextual field. However, I noticed the same contradiction that Berry (1976) notes in his research. Rather than integration, there is a differentiation of components of the art therapy space, which is characteristic of field-independent thinking.[8] The process appears to be more of a differentiative and contextualizing type and the individual is embedded in the field, as we saw in the section in chapter 4 on synaesthasia and how one child was taught Cree syllabics in the bush: the syllabics were taught as being part of the contextual field or the individual's world, and the individual elements could be easily differentiated (i.e. the syllabics, the phonetic sound, the tree, the visual element, and the individual's learning experience). Therefore, the process of learning involves contextualizing rather than decontextualizing, and it demonstrates the empathic connection the Cree people have with the natural world. When the individual is embedded in the field, the individual becomes empowered both because of the emphasis placed on the active role played by the individual – which is what occurs in the art therapy space – and because embeddedness is a metonymic evocation of the several players that are part of the composite self. Thus, there is a reliance on both the internal frame of reference (i.e. the individual) and the external frame of reference (i.e. the space). The template is similar for the construct of Cree identity and the development of Cree self, where both individuality and the relationship to others and the environment are stressed.

As presented in chapter 2, the problem that many of my Cree patients face is in identifying themselves with their culture at a collective level and at a personal level. A common dilemma most of my Cree patients face is that "Cree" is not and cannot be a marker of an autonomous people (and of autonomous individuals), yet they feel it necessary in all the definitions of self. Individuals struggle to come to grips with a definition – "Cree" – that was not part of tradition and that is politicized in such a way that it has little resonance on the individual level and their sense of self. These individuals have difficulty finding an inner balance by resolving the contradictions that they have internalized. Nonetheless, for these individuals, "Cree" remains fundamental to all definitions of the self. The elements of their definitions of Cree self include ways of the past and ways of thinking that still exist today, which together make Cree individuals distinct and provide them with a sense of belonging to the Cree collectivity or cultural group.

Many Cree individuals become entangled in the politicized discourse. Contradictions and ambiguous notions surface and these individuals become caught up in the politics of selfhood. While in art therapy, the Crees who fall victim to this stress are able to reflect, give form to the tension by understanding it, disentangle themselves from politicized notions, and ground themselves in their own notions of Cree composite self. In the end, they are better able to engage in the construction of modern self. The Cree self and the Euro-Canadian self are not necessarily opposing rhetorics where the former is relational (i.e. where the definition of self is always in relation to the other) and the latter individuated. The Cree self somehow combines both the relational and the individuated selves because the individual does not only exist in definite relationships to other selves. The Cree self is partly constituted by the process of interaction with others as well as being an autonomous self that is distinct from other selves, human and non-human. Cree people perceive an autonomous, healed self not as one that is more individuated or more relational but one that is balanced in both regards. Moreover, selfhood is perceived as more of an imaginative and reflective process than a rigid and static product, placing emphasis on the individual's active role in the self-making process. Another aspect is that the "incomplete self" becomes whole in relationship to the transcendental via animals. Foucault's insight is relevant here: "From the idea that self is not given to us, I think that there is only one practical consequence: we have to create ourselves as a work of art" (1984, 350–1).

This study could be recognized as a person-centred ethnography demonstrating how Cree individuals are not passive vehicles of their culture but rather self-conscious and active selves sharing a cultural identity. Inevitably, my patient-centred approach in psychotherapy has led to the creation of a person-centred ethnography. Exploring the Cree self within the framework of Cree cultural identity and through my Cree patients' and informants' narratives, I have discovered an interdependent relationship between Cree self and identity, where the two are mutually implicated. Epstein's definition of identity is relevant here, describing identity as representing "the process by which the person seeks to integrate his [or her] various statuses and roles, as well as his [or her] diverse experiences, into a coherent image of self" (1978, 101). Cree cultural identity is in constant flux and the Cree self is the reflexive centre of the individual, which could be seen as a relatively stable point. What my patients seek through therapy is that coherent sense of self. When the contradictions that surround them in the socio-cultural realm are internalized, the result is an imbalanced sense of self. These individuals experience the tension between being like and being the Other, or, as Taussig (1993) would define it, between sameness and alterity. Cree experience this as an identity crisis. For instance, Luke, my nine-year-old Cree patient, had created an "Indian mask" (as he called it) (figure 6.1).

He wore it throughout the session and then removed it at the end, saying that none of his friends would like it and he only wanted to wear it while in art therapy. Luke was the only Cree boy in the residential treatment unit and he experienced a strong sense of alienation. Also, before coming to Montreal for treatment, Luke had not been allowed to go to the bush, where his parents lived throughout most of the year. During his two-year treatment, he was able to eventually develop self-worth and an inner sense of stability, and to engage in "mimesis," registering both sameness and difference, being accepted by his peers both in Montreal and his Cree community as "one of them," as well as accepting his distinct traits (a hearing-impaired child, a Cree individual from the north). "Creating stability from this instability is no small task, yet all identity formation is engaged in this habitually bracing activity in which the issue is not so much staying the same, but maintaining sameness through alterity" (Taussig 1993, 129).

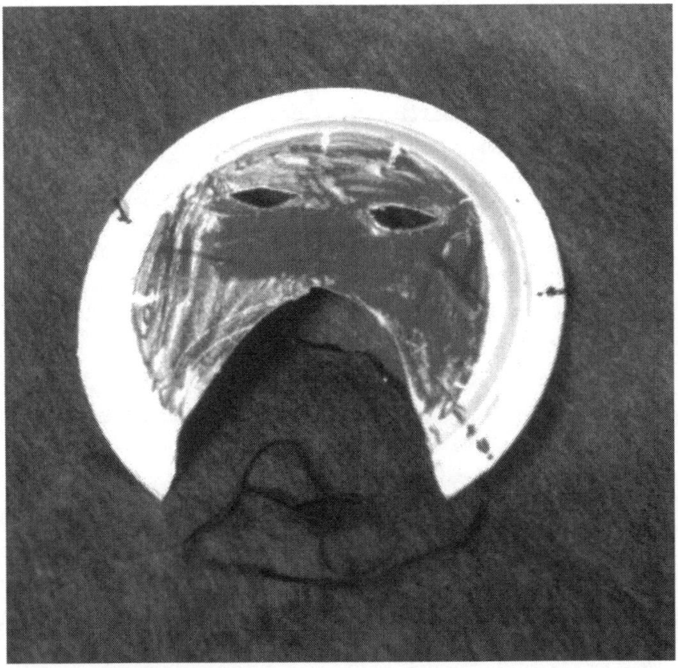

Figure 6.1 Luke's Indian mask

I also discovered that the Cree notion of self is not that different from my own. I have noted more similarities than differences, and the dichotomous split between Western self and Cree (non-Western) self was not predominant. I did not find an unbounded, unintegrated, "non-Western" type self where individual interests are subordinated "to the good of the collectivity." Instead I found in both my Cree patients and informants a strong sense of personal autonomy and a need to balance individual autonomy and social practicality or responsibility. In fact, Cree ethos appears to stress independence and individuality. I agree with Sökefeld (1999) that it may be useful to try a paradigm of similarity for conceiving others' selves rather than one of difference. However, I believe that such examination should be done in a cautious manner. Also, the anthropological study of self should not be seen as an alternative to society. As Cohen claims, "the rehabilitation of the self in social science ... proposes a view of society as composed of and by self conscious individuals" (1994, 192). I feel that in providing my Cree patients with a space to express their notions of self, as a clinician and an anthropologist, I am modestly contributing to the decolonization of the human subject. In the art therapy sanctuary, these individuals recapture, reformulate, and give meaning to their sense of self. In addition, this study exemplifies an ethnographic engagement with the Cree sense of place experienced in art therapy, a place that is highly charged with symbolic significance due to their sense of self being embedded within it.

BECOMING AN ANTHROPOLOGIST

During the process of writing this ethnography, what often emerged in the foreground of my consciousness was a piece of wisdom from a Cree elder that I find quite valuable. He emphatically said to me: "All scholarly works by Whitemen on Native people are biased by nature and are more about your own cultural views than about our own." This reminded me of Rosaldo's warning to anthropologists to remain aware of our ethnocentric projection and that "our concern with the individuals and with their hidden inner selves may well be features of *our* world of action and belief – itself to be explained and not assumed as the foundation of cross-cultural study" (1984, 147; emphasis in the original). As an ethnographer, I admit that I began with writing abstract general locutions like "among the Cree it is believed…". This did not accurately depict the slice of Cree reality I work with, and therefore I decided to accord primacy to the "selves" I interacted with. I concentrated on the "image-ful particularity" manifested by my patients and my interactions with them (Taussig 1993, 16). I have attempted to give my patients and informants a voice in this ethnography, which is essentially about their notions of self, by re-presenting their narratives and artwork. I attempted to create a relationship with the ideas of the Cree individuals and my framings as a clinician and anthropologist. Interestingly, this process is similar to that of listening to storytelling as described by Lotman (1990). According to Lotman the listener of the myth transforms the story he/she is acquiring into texts of his/her consciousness. As anthropologists, we offer interpretations of interpretations, or stories about stories and views about views (Geertz 1995).

I believe too that the inevitable starting point for my interpretation of another's selfhood is my own sense of self (Cohen 1994). My clinical work and fieldwork continue to provide me with a heightened self-awareness, especially in regards to my role as a healer. My Cree patients and informants have facilitated my own self-discovery process as a healer. Before then I saw myself as a therapist, an artist, and a teacher. I was aware that something unique was going on in the art therapy service I was providing because of the continuous successes I as well as others had noted. In the Cree community, the word soon spread from northern Quebec to northwestern Ontario and Manitoba. I would explain these successes by saying that they had to do with the alternative approach of using art to facilitate emotional expression. My colleagues in art therapy and psychiatry would agree with me. The focus was rarely on my gifts, talents, or capacities, and more on external factors such as the artwork, the art process, Cree culture, etc. I myself would focus on the artwork created in art therapy as the key to entering my Cree patients' world. Now I am looking at my role in this process, moving beyond the artwork alone and reflecting on the dynamics that allowed me to enter their world and help them create a space that became meaningful to them.

My Cree patients and informants would often encourage me to focus on my own cultural identity and how my life experiences have formed me. When they realized I was not Cree nor Aboriginal, many were interested in knowing more about my Italian cultural heritage. A Cree elder actually encouraged me to bring my healing "gift" to my "own people." I heeded his advice and recently began working in an Italian community hospital in Montreal. Also, many of my Cree informants told me to include myself in this ethnography. With all the anthropological research done on the Cree people, they unanimously felt that the works were devoid of truthful interactions between the anthropologist and the people and rarely showed how the anthropologist gained such knowledge. My informants felt that most research on the Cree people was divorced from the individual, that is, from the anthropologist writing the work and his/her relationships with the "informants," and so they encouraged me to include descriptions of my interactions with them – after all, my ethnography remains a work about my interpretations of their life experiences. As I mentioned earlier, I am operating within a postmodern sensibility by including myself in this ethnography, yet it is not necessarily just about me.

As a clinician, when I moved beyond the image of the stoic psychotherapist by sharing bits of my own self with them, my Cree patients transcended their emotional reserve. My affinity and humanity have led me to witness the profound tragedies and triumphs of many Aboriginal people, both on the individual and collective levels. As I mentioned in chapter 3, they also appear more sensitive to what I am doing as compared to my Euro-Canadian patients and have given me the title of "healer" or *minwachihiwaw.* They helped me discover my gift to help others heal in the way that I attentively listen, help them reframe their emotional and spiritual experiences, and encourage a dialogue between us. Moreover, I am able to heal because they acknowledge me as being part of their collectivity and believe that through our dialogic creation I help them form a healthy composite self.

What initially began as uncertain dialogue between cultural traditions, awkward greetings, and doubts developed into a sense of comfort and faith as my patients and I negotiated a sense of place to heal their fragmented sense of self. As this ethnography illustrates, our interaction patterns – the narratives and emotional discourse framed by both the art therapy rhetorical structure and mythopoetic Cree thought – have been instrumental in the creation of art therapy as a ritual space.

I realize how my knowledge of my Cree informants is primarily a matter of sociality, that is, my knowledge evolves through my exchanges with them. My experience is akin to that of Jackson, who writes, "the possibility of anthropology is born when the other recognizes my humanity, and on the strength of this recognition incorporates me into his world, giving me food and shelter, bestowing upon me a name … I am literally incorporated into his world, and it is on the basis of this incorporation and my reciprocal response to it that I begin to gain a knowledge of that world" (1995, 119).

What began as an unfamiliar setting essentially called for my own self-reflection. Beliefs and values are often taken for granted because they are so unconscious, and they can become foreign because we do not reflect upon them. For instance, a belief I had was that animals were subordinate to humans and a relationship between the two was meaningful if the animal became a pet. With my Cree patients and friends, I was acculturated to a reality where animals play a significant role in communication and the formation of self. Although I have yet to have a communicative experience with an animal in the bush, I have developed an appreciation for this reality and it has become less strange to me because I have listened attentively to so many encounters. As I described throughout this study, my Cree informants led me to cultivate my own subjective meaning of reality, especially in relation to my experience in the bush. When I first came face to face with a caribou, Sid, a Cree elder, understood why I was shaking like a leaf and later ran into the van, crippled with fear. I later apologized for stalling our excursion. All Sid said, with his dry sense of humour, was that it was not yet my time for my animal encounter!

During this fieldwork, often what appeared foreign was eventually made familiar. For instance, when I first discovered the notion of synaesthasia, I immediately saw its relevance among my Cree informants and their style of perception. In my research, I noticed how both the Cree "cognitive style" and synaesthasia were implicitly categorized as distinct styles of perception. In both "styles" we find a definite interrelationship between affect, perception, sensation, and the construction of meaning. The more I researched the concept of synaesthasia and discussed it thoroughly with anthropologists George Fulford and Richard Preston, the more I saw links to Cree reality and the more I realized that it is a process I engage in myself at times. One time in Vermont with a hearing-impaired friend of mine, surrounded by trees and the beautiful sound of rustling leaves, I wondered to myself how she could experience the sound, as it was something I found so spectacular. I closed my eyes and allowed myself to experience the sound. I then told her to place "Rice Crispies" cereal in her mouth and experience the texture. To me, this tactile sensation came closest to the sound of the rustling leaves.

I agree with Tuan (1993), who argues that the synaesthetic tendency is commonplace as the blending of senses is so habitual that we take it completely for granted. Cross-modal sensory associations are often used to facilitate memory (Fulford 2000a). Such multisensorial experience is probably a process we engage in unconsciously or without labelling it. The Cree people I work with also do not necessarily label this process as "synaesthetic" or as multisensorial. As with the notions of art and self, they do not have specific terms to describe entities or processes that for them are simply part of their life experience. As Bob told me, "the terms spirituality, tradition, belief, family, storytelling can't be defined separately. They are all part of a way of life." The fact that the Cree individuals I work with may not have similar terms or predefined categories does not mean they do not experience such processes or possess similar notions of such entities.

During these past fifteen years working with the Cree people, I experienced first-hand, as Napier eloquently claims, that "strangers within our midst are, indeed, the strangest of all – not because they

Figure 6.2 Luke's heart drawing no. 1

are so alien, but because they are so close to us. ... They cannot be completely exotic, for, were they so, we could not recognize them" (1992, 147). My Cree patients and informants and I created a connection between my world and theirs and we discovered degrees of familiarity. My experience also concords with Shweder's (1990) observations; he notes that our inability to get beyond appearances of reality with methods of science or rules of logic doesn't mean we stop trying to imagine what is real to another.

Both my fieldwork and clinical work are characterized by a dialogic exchange, where my patients, informants and myself gain knowledge and insights from each other. In such an interactive and dialogically conceived-type therapeutic encounter, I am recognizing the reciprocal influence between therapist and patient. This reminds me of a drawing directive I gave to Luke during our first session together. I asked him to draw about people doing something together, which was part of a diagnostic art therapy procedure that I was being trained to use. Luke's response was to write his name and mine, each enclosed in a box-like form, and then draw a heart, divided in half. He told me that he was going to show me how to colour in my half of the heart (figure 6.2).

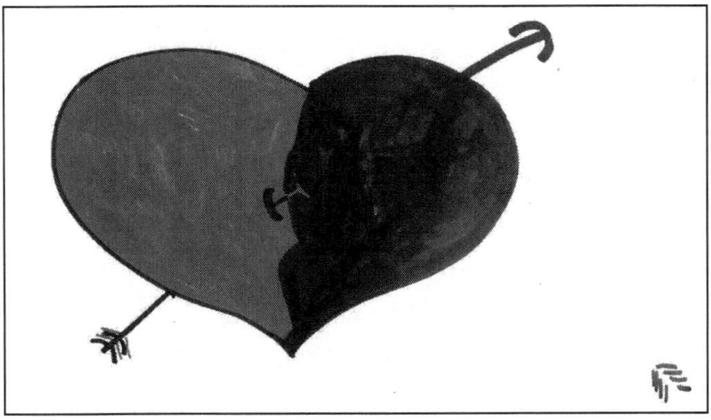

Figure 6.3 Luke's heart drawing no. 2

Luke gave me the black marker while he used the red, and I followed his directions with no hesitation. Interestingly, my clinical supervisor reprimanded me for engaging in the art-making process with Luke because it encourages enmeshment and not separate autonomous selves. Now, in hindsight, I understand the reprimand, which exemplifies a Western culture-bound value (i.e. separate selves). Given my experience with Cree patients, I also better comprehend Luke's intention and understanding of the directive. It was not necessarily a misunderstanding but rather his interpretation of the healing through art as an interactive encounter. I did not get the sense that Luke was losing his sense of self in asking me to draw with him. In fact, he was acknowledging my separate sense of self in giving me a separate space to colour in and a different colour. In his own way, Luke was gravitating toward me to help him make sense of the inner turmoil he was feeling. A Cree elder in Luke's community informed me that red symbolizes a visionary or feeling state and black symbolizes reason. According to the elder, Luke, in giving me the black marker, was symbolically asking me to help him make sense of his feelings so that together we formed a healthy, composite self. Interestingly, during one of our last sessions, Luke asked that we draw together "one last time." Once again he drew the heart, this time it appears with more form, and Luke suggested we interchange the markers. He noted emphatically: "don't forget to leave a space in the middle to make the connection" (figure 6.3). The heart became symbolic of a relationship that facilitated Luke's healing process towards a more balanced sense of self engaged with the Other.

As art therapy makes inner sense to the Cree people I work with, their mythopoetic thought and how it is used in their healing process now makes sense to me. A female Cree elder who was working with me as an interpreter recently told a mother of a young girl I was seeing in art therapy, "*aspayimotam miyoapatisiou*," which is translated as "have faith, she works with art."

Notes

CHAPTER ONE

1 See Ferrara (1991, 1998).

2 Throughout this study I use the term "patient" rather than "client" in reference to the individuals who come to see me in the clinical context. It is a matter of preference and it is the term that the Cree people I work with use. Thus far, I have seen approximately 1000 Cree patients, mostly for short-term therapy and several for long-term therapy (i.e. for a period of one to two years). In terms of statistics, 60 percent of my patients in Northern Quebec region (i.e. from all nine Cree communities) are male and 40 percent are female.

3 See Ferrara (1999, 1996, 1992).

4 In relation to art among Cree people, a relevant study with a different focus is Fulford's 1994 structural analysis of drawings of a group of Cree children from northeastern Ontario. Fulford illustrates how art is used as a natural and silent form of communication, and he claims that the children's drawings have a narrative function, containing elements such as characters, a setting, plot, and theme, and that they serve as a form of self-expression (40).

5 Throughout this ethnography, I will be making a distinction between my patients and the individuals I have met and worked with outside the clinical setting, whom I will refer to as my informants. Both my patients and informants have provided me with valuable insights on Cree values and beliefs.

6 There is a large body of research that has identified "healable" personality types in terms of Western-style therapy (see Ferrara 1999).

7 Rabinow and Sullivan also direct their attention to this important point: "our capacity to understand is rooted in our own self-definitions, hence in what we are. What we are is a self-interpreting and self-defining animal" (1979, 6). As anthropologists, we offer interpretations of interpretations.

8 As coined by Anderson, "imagined community" refers to collective identity that can involve diversity, real and imagined. In the Cree case, it would refer to the Cree people's attempts to create a Cree collective cultural identity, relying on essentialized and reconstructed notions of history (Anderson 1991; Boyarin 1994).

9 Colonialism refers to the First Nation peoples' experience of being forced to accept a centralized authority to which they have all been subordinated. First Nations have had to remould themselves in the Euro-Canadian cultural patten, leading to the destruction of their indigenous systems of thought and ways of life (Dickason 1997, 13). The Canadian colonial power structure continues to this day, with the nation's unremitting desire to exploit indigenous lands (Alfred 1999, 98).

10 Discursive practice refers to the communication that emerges in the situational context of therapy that is often stimulated by the artwork created by the patient.

11 According to one of my informants, storytelling is used as an instrument of knowledge to promote intellectual and emotional well-being, or *miyupimaatisiiun* (see Adelson 2000; Cruikshank 1990) both at the personal and collective levels. The telling of and listening to a story is both a spiritual and emotional experience because you are involved in doing something meaningful, *chistaamaawin*.

12 The syncretic quality of myth relates to how myth involves the coalescence of contradictory elements of the metaphysical dimension in its attempt to explain it. The concrete form of myth relates to the artistic images that myth expresses (Metelinsky 1998).

13 See White and Epstein (1990, 217), who argue for a therapy that incorporates narrative means "as an instrument of liberty" and self-awareness.

14 See Kerby (1991, 4).

CHAPTER TWO

1 The nine Cree communities in northern Quebec include Chisasibi, Nemaska, Mistassini, Wemindji, Waswanapi, Waskaganish, Ouje-Bougamou, East Main, and Whapmagoostui.

2 For more on the use of traditional healers and the continued access to traditional medicine, I suggest Waldram (1990) and Gregory's (1989) work.

Even though they are describing Cree communities in western Canada, some similarities can be drawn to the northern Quebec Crees.

3 Many Euro-Canadians consider the traditional lifestyle unprofitable, yet they are using a Western model of the economy in this interpretation. The economic profit model does not apply to Cree values. Profit is defined in more traditional terms, as a way of life that is healthy and balanced in both natural and human communities.

4 It is important to note that I am not an expert in the field of Cree social organization and this study is not about this. I want to highlight the differences that are often noted by my patients and informants in terms of kinship values then and now.

5 The term "brotherhood" relates to a network of partnerships as a whole hunting-trapping unit, and it is used metaphorically to represent an idealized solidarity of people who base important choices in the present on the history of past working partnerships; for example, members of one's brotherhood are sons and daughters of people who worked with one's parents. Naturally, the parents see their partnerships as just that, partnerships. From their children's viewpoint, however, these partnerships appear as close and even fundamental bonds that produce kinship, hence Turner and Wertman's decision to use the word "brotherhood" for the resulting networks. Turner and Wertman are explicit that the people in brotherhoods are not genealogical brothers, nor are they considered as such by the Shamattawa Crees. This model was also used in other studies by some of Turner's students (see Lanoue 1992; Trott 1982) in non-Cree contexts. Despite obvious differences with the Shamattawa Crees, they confirmed that while "brotherhoods" is a useful word to describe the close relationships that characterize these networks, in no case were these feelings of solidarity interpreted by informants as indicative of an actual genealogical bond. Such kinship ties may be present – some people in brotherhoods are indeed genealogical brothers and sisters – but these are considered unimportant or secondary by informants describing their society and its social categories.

6 For more on this notion of animism, which is a common element found in various Native American religions, see Tooker and Sturtevant (1979).

7 During the contact period, the Europeans mangled and mispronounced some difficult names. According to McFarlane and Haimila (1999), the best example of this was with the Cree people of the James Bay region, who were originally named Kenistenaag: "The French first mispronounced their name as Kristinaux and then shortened the misnomer to Cris, which the English then rendered Cree" (71). I believe that this

misnomer of "Kristinaux" was also related to the movement toward Christianizing the people who were referred to as "Indian savages."

8 Both Rogers (1963) and Morantz (1983) address that the definition of the term "band" is obscured and used loosely in anthropological literature. Also, both authors agree that the band was most probably not a fur trade development and that such a group descended from a pre-contact group that used to assemble seasonally. However, as noted by both Rogers and Morantz, there is insufficient prehistoric information to conclude this. Morantz (1983, 99) prefers the use of the term "macro-group" over "band." As I stated in an earlier endnote, I am not interested in addressing Cree social organization per se in this study. However, because of the immediate presence of the collectivity in the construction of self, I believe that it is important to address the nature of the band and the Cree notion of collectivity.

9 It was believed that residential schools would accelerate the assimilation process by removing children from their homes and their communities, usually for extended periods of time (Dickason 1997). They began in late 1930s and were shut down in the late 1960s (Frideres 1998). See Miller (1996) for a history of Native residential schools.

10 This agreement is considered Canada's first modern aboriginal treaty and was one of the first steps taken by the federal government and by aboriginal people to establish self-government (Report of the Cree-Naskapi Commission, 1994).

11 See Ferrara (1999).

12 While indigenous definitions have pre-contact origins, "indigenous" is a term that better accommodates over three centuries of influence from relations with Europeans. It is not "pre-contact" definitions of the self that are salient in Cree imaginations and that the Crees feel unable to use, but rather indigenous definitions nearer to hand historically, as embodied in and communicated by parents and grandparents.

13 The Crees of Quebec are in close contact with Euro-Canadians, specifically Quebecers, many of whom live in the Cree communities and in neighbouring cities. Both Cree and Inuit people live in the community of Whapmagoostui at Great Whale River.

14 My intention here is not to offer a thorough analysis of pan-Indianism but to accentuate that it is a political discourse. For a more elaborate description of this movement see Lanoue's 1992 work.

15 Sampson claims that sociocentrism or "ensembled individualism" is less familiar to Westerners as a form of individualism, yet paradoxically it has

greater worldwide presence. It is wrongly assumed that freedom, autonomy, and independence require self-contained individualism for their realization (Sampson 1988). However, ensembled individualism may better realize these values because when an individual's "sense of self is defined through relationship and connection, achievements will occur, not by separate actors seeking somehow to mesh their behavior together, but rather from thoroughly interdependent actors whose very design for being includes working on behalf of larger interests" (21).

16 Dunning addresses this problem of Native people acting as "cultural brokers," or what he calls "the marginal man," in their experience of acculturation. Dunning explains that this person is in the position of a middleman, representing the Western world and playing the role of effecting change in his ethnic community (1959, 122).

17 See Lanoue (2000, 2001).

CHAPTER THREE

1 Kinesics relates to the study of bodily movements, gestures, and facial expressions as ways of communication.

2 See Basso (1970), Darnell (1981), Phillips (1976), and Spielmann (1998).

3 During the past fifteen years I have also worked with Mohawk, Ojibwa, Abenaki, and Inuit people.

4 Speech acts relate to how speech is regulated and structured. For a more developed description of the speech act theory, see Austin (1962) and Searle (1969).

5 The significance of the role of the third person is a unique feature of Cree grammar as well as other Algonquian languages (e.g. Ojibwa), and it is referred to as obviation (Dahlstrom 1996, 121). The more peripheral third persons are the marked obviative forms, which relate to the point of view of who is doing the seeing rather than who is doing the speaking (Spielmann 1998).

6 Bodily expressions include the physical or biological sensations, body image, and how the body is symbolized in a given society.

7 This line of argument, showing how emotions are used as instruments in the negotiation of relationships, has been richly developed by Lutz and Abu-Lughod (1990).

8 By somatization, I mean the belief that repressed emotions will emerge and harm the body by causing stress. Neuroses are psychic blockages that the individual may overcome by verbalizing his/her fears or conflicts.

9 On the relationship between self and the social context, see Shweder and Bourne (1982); Heelas and Lock (1981); and Lock and Scheper-Hughes (1990).
10 On the concept of politics of identity, see T. Turner (1995) and Parkin (1985).
11 Corporeal existence or practice is also referred to as "habitus" (Bourdieu 1977) and "embodied sociality" (Csordas 1993).
12 Anna Freud (1946) outlines a number of different defense mechanisms, including displacement, which relates to impulses and feelings that are unconsciously transferred from the original source or person to a less threatening source.
13 A bushman is an individual who lives mostly in the bush as a hunter and fisherman. This term is used by many Crees, and it has very positive associations.
14 This emphasis on pragmatic flexibility also manifests itself in the form of female healers.
15 In the sweat lodge, or *mitutisaan*, which is used for healing purposes, hot coals are placed at the centre of a wigwam (or teepee) and people sit inside and express their concerns, problems, and/or emotions in the hope of gaining insight. The sweat lodge was used in the past to cleanse the individual both physically and symbolically in preparation for hunting (Tanner 1979). I have noticed that in the past ten years or so sweat lodges are being used more and more by aboriginal people for healing purposes.

CHAPTER FOUR

1 Ingold (1996) strongly recommends that Westerners use the hunter-gatherer reality set, such as that of the Crees', to re-evaluate their own way of thinking and living. Brody, too, believes that "there are lessons to be learned from the hunter-gatherer world that go to the core of who we are as human beings. … There may also be lessons and explanations of a kind, for some of the malaise and sense of inadequacy that afflict so many of us" (2000, 8).
2 Nuttall (1992, 75) describes a similar process of personal identity development among the Inuit people in Greenland.
3 For more on Vico's theories on myth and his notion of "poetic wisdom," see O'Neill (1994), Danesi (1993), and Hawkes (1977).
4 These relationships usually occur among Cree males, both young and old, because traditionally this spiritual contact was between the (male) hunter and the animal. I have, however, heard from my Cree informants about

females who had similar encounters with animals when they were sent into the bush on vision quests.

5 Although Brightman's (1993) work deals with the Western Woods Crees of northern Manitoba, specifically the Rock Crees, his study on human-animal relationships is relevant to my observations of the northern Quebec Crees.

6 The Cree people form part of the linguistic group known as Algonquian, which also include the Ojibwa and the Innu. This "family" of hunting peoples spoke a dialect of what linguists refer to as the Algonquian language (McFarlane and Haimila 1999).

7 See also Brightman (1993, xii).

8 In several Cree and Ojibwa community schools in northwestern Ontario that were affected by high suicide rates, I helped the people develop programs that involved extracurricular bush or land-based activities for the students. According to the people of these communities, the programs helped decrease the suicide rates significantly.

9 As elucidated by Adelson (2000, 69), the hierarchy of power is associated with three important, interdependent elements: type of habitat, type of locomotion (four paws, flight, swim), and temporal-spatial distribution (seasonal migration).

10 In my work, I usually ask my informants' permission to record notes on their accounts of encounters with animals. Sometimes they ask that parts of the conversation remain private (see Goulet 1994b).

11 A phrase coined by Bakewell (1998), "image acts" essentially refers to the use of visual metaphors or iconic representations.

12 See Ochs and Capps (1996, 21) for a definition of narratives of personal experience.

13 The order of the figures showing Tom's artwork does not reflect the actual order he created them in. Some were created during our sessions, while others were made outside of our sessions.

14 Cree syllabics relate to a linguistic lexicon that was introduced to Cree people by the missionaries in the late nineteenth century. It is still used today.

15 According to Dann (1998, 8), there are four synaesthetic associations that occur naturally, including: (1) visual-auditory (sound-induced visual percepts); (2) tactile-visual (sight-induced sensations of touch); (3) tactile-auditory (sound-induced sensations of touch); and (4) kinaesthetic-olfactory (smell-induced bodily sensations).

16 It is important to note that, although I have noted synaesthetic elements in Cree perception styles manifested by my patients and informants, synaesthasia appears to be more of an individual rather than social process (see Fulford 2000a).

17 See Marks (1990), who argues that metaphor and other tropes such as metonymy are extensions of cross-modal similarities.

CHAPTER FIVE

1 Interestingly, this capacity to create memoryscapes resembles Yates' theory on the art of memory, which, according to Yates, is an art that "seeks to memorise through a technique of impressing 'places' and 'images' on memory" (1966, xi). I found a parallel between landscape, memoryscape, and Yates' discussion of memory loci drawing on the mnemonic techniques of Greek and Roman orators. The techniques described by Yates draw on the use of visual templates (i.e. the mental image of a familiar room where key ideas can be temporarily stored) and might be compared with the way in which Cree people name the landscape and code stories associated with the names into the image of the place. Thus, instead of storing key ideas in an imaginary room, a Cree person may encode the landscape in a series of names that themselves constitute a mental map (see Brody 1981, 37, 177).

2 These four drawings, created by a forty-year-old Cree woman, are an example of the Ulman Personality Assessment Procedure (UPAP). I often use this procedure in pre-, mid-, and post-treatment stages. In the first drawing the patient is asked to create a free drawing, and this woman chose to draw symbols of the bush. The second one involves a kinaesthetic-movement drawing, where the patient creates arm movements in the air and then records them on paper. This woman's response was to draw the human figure doing the movements, which is a common response among my Cree patients (see Ferrara 1999). The third is a scribble drawing, where the patient is asked to close his/her eyes, scribble on the paper, and then open his/her eyes and look for an image in the scribble and develop it through. In the fourth drawing, the patient may either create a free drawing like the first or a scribble like the third. Although she did return to a stereotypic form (a heart), this woman chose the scribble again, showing her readiness to engage in spontaneous expression. See Ulman and Dachinger (1975) for more information on this art therapy assessment, and Ferrara (1999) for a demonstration on how it was used in a cross-cultural study on emotional expression.

3 Moore (1990) provides a thorough analysis of Paul Ricoeur's theories on narratives and self-reflection.

4 Also relevant here is Lacan's (1949) discussion on the mirror image, where he shows how psychoanalysts have brought out the major role that this

image plays in the child's personality development. The artwork in art therapy, like the "mirror stage," creates a sense of permanency, and a primitive notion of self is internalized.

5 Gusdorf (1980) also discusses the importance of the mirror in the literary genre of autobiography, where moments of reflection are created. This accords with my description of therapeutic activity as autobiographical.

6 Gerhardt and Stinson (1996, 456) note the recent trend in psychotherapy toward more interactive and dialogically conceived accounts of the therapeutic encounter, and they recognize this as a paradigm shift in psychotherapy.

7 Lévi-Strauss (1963, 180–3) also found links between shamanistic rituals and psychoanalysis; for example, in both the goal is to help the patient integrate contradictory elements. He also noted some distinct differences; for example, the shaman feels and speaks for the silent patient, whereas in psychoanalysis, the patient talks to the listening therapist and relives the initial situation that caused the disturbance. Dow (1986) also addresses how shamanism and Western psychotherapy invoke similar psychological processes.

8 See Pred on how people reproduce and transform social and spatial structures. Pred argues that social and spatial structures are dialectically entwined, adding that "not only is the spatial socially produced, but social life, the engagement of people in their 'lifeworlds,' is always spatially dependent" (1990, 10). Bell (1992, 89) also notes that ritual forms of behaviour define, model, and communicate social relations.

9 It is important to note that the Crees do not themselves make the distinction between sacred and secular; this is ethnocentric on my part.

10 Here, I am reminded of the psychoanalyst Melanie Klein (1961) and her observation that the therapy she provided was an island of calm for troubled children, but at the end of the session, the child had to return to his/her dysfunctional family to continue muddling through a dysfunctional world. I elaborate more on this notion of containment in therapy further on in this section.

11 V. Turner (1967, 27–32) discusses another property that will not be addressed here, which relates to the unification of disparate significata. Turner also differentiates between dominant and instrumental symbols, where in the latter the meaning is context-dependent. Instrumental symbols can be found in art therapy as well, as in theme-related artwork, where, for instance, the patient is asked to draw a family picture. I have limited my discussion to the properties of the dominant ritual symbol that appear relevant to the art therapy process.

12 This image of the medicine wheel is highly syncretic and heavily influenced by pan-Indian symbolism.

13 Although, as noted by Brass (1999, 45), there exists sparse historic and ethnographic information on the indigenous practice of the medicine wheel, it is seen as a pervasive and culturally universal symbol and vehicle of healing. The medicine wheel could also be considered a pan-Indian symbol.

14 Victor Turner's development of the liminality notion is seen by Rosaldo as "a concept designed to 'recover' energy and affect within the context of a structuralist perspective" (1984, 151n2). Turner also recognized the importance of embodied knowledge as a significant way in which cultural models, such as rituals, bridge the gap between personal experience and social convention (Shore 1996).

15 This will be developed further in the subsequent section on the metonymic links between art therapy and the bush.

16 Dow (1986, 59) defines the notion of "mythic world" as an individual's culturally specific beliefs, metaphors, and idioms.

17 This statement was expressed by both my female and male patients and informants.

18 See Casey (1996) for more on emplaced experiences.

19 The binary oppositions of these properties respectively are complexity, intermittent reference to mystical powers, state, secularity, and speech. Turner outlines several more discriminations (1969, 106–7). I have selected these particular ones for the purpose of my analysis.

20 For more on the Cree experience of the non-verbal exchange with animals in the bush see Preston (2002).

21 For a cross-cultural analysis of Euro-Canadian and Crees' uses of art therapy see Ferrara (1999).

22 I believe that Ingold (1996) is borrowing from Heidegger's notion of dwelling, which deals with how individuals perceive and apprehend space. According to Heidegger, "spaces receive their essential being from particular localities and not from 'space' itself" (1977, 332). Dwelling consists in the lived relationships that people maintain with places (Heidegger 1977). Heidegger's conception of "being-there" appears quite similar to the Cree notion of "I am just there," in that they both possess a spatial-temporal quality and allude to the existential relationship between self and place.

23 Shweder's (1990) concept of "intentional world" relates to the process of creating mental representations.

24 Hallowell's anthropological studies of the Ojibwa people of northern Ontario is relevant to my study here. Hallowell refers to the non-human

components as "personified natural objects" (1966, 275) and defines them elsewhere as "living entities who are integrally related to human beings … and constantly interact with them" (1963, 272). Preston (1975, 239) also notes that Hallowell's distinction between humans and other-than-human persons corresponds to Cree perception. Preston adds that other-than-human persons are viewed as "inhabitants of the [Cree] hunter's world."

25 For a Cree dictionary, see *Cree Lexicon* (1987).

26 The concept of "moral landscape" refers to ethical lessons that are mapped on the land and that offer the Apache people constant cues on how they live (Basso, 1996).

CHAPTER SIX

1 The process of deriving meaning from repetition and rhythm is also a feature of traditional chants and drum songs found throughout Algonquian cultures (see Fulford 1994; Scott 1996; Preston 2002).

2 Hobsbawn (1983, 4) describes the process of "inventing traditions" in modern societies as a form of ritualization. While I do not believe that my Cree patients are engaged in "inventing traditions," in relation to their art therapy ritualized experience they seem to be reformulating aspects of their Cree self as a strategy of survival.

3 Using Tarasoff's (1980, 15) terminology, which appears relevant to the Crees of Quebec, this would be referred to as the cultural process of persistence; as the Cree culture changes due to the process of acculturation, certain elements prevail over a long period of time, such as bush lifeways.

4 Similarly, Ewing's (1990) Pakistani informants experienced this strategy to create self-representations.

5 "Habitus" relates to the routine practice within which people experience the world around them (Bourdieu 1977).

6 Abu-Lughod (1986) provides an ethnography on Bedouin love poetry as a traditional-type discourse that informs the social actors how they can think and feel.

7 According to Burke, "rhetoric is the art of persuasion" (1973, 46). Cree animal-doctor discourse can be seen as an act of persuasion or inducement to action, which in this case would be for me to listen attentively to the patient's interests or what Burke calls "symbol-using entity" (i.e. animal-doctors).

8 Berry (1976) also notes that the Crees, like many hunter-gatherers, demonstrate highly developed spatial ability, which is associated with right hemispheric lateralization. However, whether field-independence among hunter-gatherers is associated with right hemispheric lateralization or with long-term ecological adaptations is not known. Interestingly, art-making is related to relative right hemispheric dominance (Edwards 1979). The correlations between art-making, spatial ability, and Cree cognitive style definitely require further research. I believe that by defining the process as being biological or neuropsychological or as a cultural construction is limiting and uni-dimensional. I view the art-making process as more multifaceted, combining all these dimensions.

References

Abu-Lughod, L. 1986. *Veiled sentiments: Honor and poetry in a Bedouin society.* Berkeley: University of California Press.

Adelson, N. 2000. *'Being alive well': Health and the politics of Cree well-being.* Toronto: University of Toronto Press.

– 2001. Gathering knowledge: Reflections on the anthropology of identity, Aboriginality, and the annual gatherings in Whapmagoostui, Quebec. In C.H. Scott, ed., *Aboriginal autonomy and development in northern Quebec and Labrador*, 289–303. Vancouver: University of British Columbia Press.

Alfred, T. 1999. *Peace, power, righteousness.* Don Mills: Oxford University Press.

American Art Therapy Association (AATA). 2001. Newsletter, Spring Issue.

Anderson, B. 1991. *Imagined communities: Reflections on the spread of nationalism.* Second edition. London: Verso.

Atkinson, H.B., and G. Magonet, eds. 1990. *The James Bay experience.* Quebec: Government of Quebec.

Augé, M. 1995. *Non-places: Introduction to an anthropology of supermodernity.* J. Howe, trans. London: Verso.

Austin, J.L. 1962. *How to do things with words.* Cambridge: Harvard University Press.

Bachelard, G. 1969. *The poetics of space.* M. Jolas, trans. Boston: Beacon Press.

Bakewell, L. 1998. Image acts. *American Anthropologist* 100, 22–32.

Basso, K.H. 1970. "To give up on words": Silence in Western Apache culture. *Southwestern Journal of Anthropology* 26, 213–30.

– 1996. Wisdom sits in places. In S. Feld and K.H. Basso, eds., *Senses of place*, 53–90. Santa Fe: School of American Research Press.

Battaglia, D., ed. 1995. *Rhetorics of self-making.* Berkeley: University of California Press.

Bearskin, S. and C. Dumont, 1991. The Cree Board of Health and Social Services of James Bay: The First Twelve Years – 1978–1990. In B. Postl el al., eds., *Circumpolar Health 90: Proceedings of the 8th International Congress*, 123–5. Winnipeg: University of Manitoba Press.

Bell, C. 1992. *Ritual theory, ritual practice*. Oxford: Oxford University Press.

– 1997. *Ritual: Perspectives and dimensions*. Oxford: Oxford University Press.

Berry, J.W. 1976. *Human ecology and cognitive style: Comparative studies in cultural and psychological adaptation*. Beverly Hills: Sage.

Berry, J.W. and J.A. Bennett. 1992. Cree conceptions of cognitive competence. *International Journal of Psychology*, 27, 73–88.

Besnier, N. 1990. Language and affect. *Annual Review of Anthropology*, 19, 419–51.

Bibeau, G. and E. Corin, eds. 1995. *Beyond textuality: Asceticism and violence in anthropological interpretation*. Berlin: Mouton de Gruyter.

Bierhorst, J. 1994. *The way of the earth: Native America and the environment*. New York: William Morrow.

Blacking, J., ed. 1977. *The anthropology of the body*. London: Academic Press.

Boyarin, J., ed. 1994. *Remapping memory: The politics of timespace*. Minneapolis: University of Minnesota Press.

Bourdieu, P. 1977. *Outline of a theory of practice*. R. Nice, trans. Cambridge: Cambridge University Press.

Brant, C.C. 1990. Native ethics and rules of behavior. *Canadian Journal of Psychiatry*, 35, 534–9.

Brass, G.M. 1999. *Respecting "the medicines": Narrating an aboriginal identity at Nechi House*. Unpublished masters' thesis. Montreal: McGill University.

Brenneis, D.N. 1987. Talk and transformation. *Man*, 22, 499–510.

Briggs, J.L. 1970. *Never in anger*. Cambridge: Harvard University Press.

– 1987. In search of emotional meaning. *Ethos* 15, 8–15.

– 1998. *Inuit morality play: The emotional education of a three-year-old*. New Haven: Yale University Press.

Brightman, R. 1993. *Grateful prey: Rock Cree human-animal relationships*. Berkeley: University of California Press.

Brody, H. 1981. *Maps and dreams: Indians and the British Columbian frontier*. Vancouver: Douglas & McIntyre.

– 2000. *The other side of Eden: Hunters, farmers and the shaping of the world*. Vancouver: Douglas & McIntyre.

Bruner, E.M. 1986. Introduction. In V.W. Turner and E.M. Bruner, eds., *The anthropology of experience*, 3–30. Urbana: University of Illinois.

Burke, K. 1973. *The philosophy of literary form: Studies in symbolic action*. Berkeley: University of California Press.

Burridge, K. 1979. *Someone, no one. An essay on individuality.* Princeton: Princeton University Press.

Casey, E.S. 1996. How to get from space to place in a fairly short stretch of time. In S. Feld and K.H. Basso, eds., *Senses of place*, 13–52. Santa Fe: School of American Research Press.

Cohen, A. 1994. *Self-consciousness: An alternative anthropology of identity.* London: Routledge.

Coppinger, R. and W. Ryan. 1999. James Bay: Environmental considerations for building large hydroelectric dams and reservoirs in Quebec. In James F. Hornig, ed., *Social and environmental impacts of the James Bay hydroelectric project*, 41–72. Montreal: McGill-Queen's University Press.

Crapanzano, V. 1980. *Tuhami: Portrait of a Moroccan.* Chicago: The University of Chicago Press.

Cree Lexicon: Eastern James Bay Dialects 1987. Chisasibi: Cree School Board.

Cruikshank, J. 1990. *Life lived like a story: Life stories of three Yukon Native elders.* Lincoln: University of Nebraska Press.

Csordas, T.J. 1990. Embodiment as a paradigm for anthropology. *Ethos* 18, 5–47.

– 1993. Somatic modes of attention. *Cultural Anthropology* 8, 135–56.

Dahlstrom, A. 1996. Narrative structure of a Fox text. In J.D. Nichols and A.C. Ogg, eds., *Nikotwâsik iskwâhtêm, pâskihtêpayih! Studies in honor of H.C. Wolfart*, 113–62. Memoir 13, Algonquian and Iroquoian Linguistics.

Danesi, M. 1993. *Vico, metaphor and the origin of language.* Bloomington: Indiana University Press.

Dann, K.T. 1998. *Bright colors falsely seen: Synaesthasia and the search for transcendental knowledge.* New Haven: Yale University Press.

Darnell, R. 1981. Taciturnity in Native American etiquette: A Cree case. *Culture*, 1, 55–960.

– 1988. The implications of Cree interactional etiquette. In R. Darnell and M.K. Foster, eds., *Native North American interaction patterns*, 69–77. Hull: Canadian Museum of Civilization.

Desgent, J.M. and G. Lanoue. 2001. *Errances: Comment se pensent le nous et le moi dans l'espace mythique des nomades septentrionaux sekani.* Montréal: Les Erbes Rouges.

Desjarlais, R.R. 1992. *Body and emotion: The aesthetics of illness and healing in the Nepal Himalayas.* Philadelphia: University of Pennsylvania Press.

Dickason, O.P. 1997. *Canada's First Nations: A history of founding peoples from earliest times.* (2nd ed.) Toronto: Oxford University Press.

Douglas, M. 1970. *Natural symbols: Explorations in cosmology.* London: Routledge.

Dow, J. 1986. Universal aspects of symbolic healing: A theoretical synthesis. *American Anthropologist* 88, 56–69.

Dunning, R.W. 1959. Ethnic relations and the marginal man in Canada. *Human Organization* 18, 117–22.

Duran, E. and B. Duran. 1995. *Native American postcolonial psychology.* Albany: State University of New York Press.

Edwards, B. 1979. *Drawing on the right side of the brain.* New York: St Martin's Press.

Ekman, P. 1984. Expression and the nature of emotion. In K. Scherer and P. Ekman, eds., *Approaches to emotion*, 319–43. New Jersey: Lawrence Erlbaum.

Epstein, A.L. 1978. *Ethos and identity: Three studies in ethnicity.* London: Tavistock.

Erchak, G.M. 1992. *The anthropology of self and behavior.* New Brunswick: Rutgers University Press.

Ewing, K. 1990. The illusion of wholeness: Culture, self, and the experience of inconsistency. *Ethos* 18, 251–78.

Fabian, J. 1983. *Time and the other.* New York: Columbia University Press.

Farkas, C.S. 1986. Ethno-specific communication patterns: Implications for nutrition education. *Journal of Nutrition Education* 18, 99–103.

Feld, S. and K.H. Basso. eds. 1996. *Senses of place.* Santa Fe: School of American Research Press.

Feit, H. 1973. The ethno-ecology of the Waswanipi Cree: or how hunters can manage their resources. In B. Cox, ed., *Cultural ecology: Readings on the Canadian Indians and Eskimos.* Toronto: McClelland & Stewart.

– 1985. Legitimation and autonomy in James Bay Cree responses to Hydro-Electric development. In N. Dyck, ed., *Indigenous peoples and the Nation-State: Fourth World politics in Canada, Australia and Norway.* St John's: Institute of Social and Economic Research, Memorial University of Newfoundland.

– 1986. Hunting and the quest for power: The James Bay Cree and Whitemen in the Twentieth Century. In R.B. Morrison and C.R. Williams, eds., *Native Peoples: The Canadian Experience*, 171–207. Toronto: McClelland & Stewart.

– 1991. Gifts of the land: Hunting territories, guaranteed incomes and the construction of social relations in James Bay Cree society. In N. Peterson and T. Matsuyama, eds., *Senri Ethnological Studies* 30, 207–23. Osaka: National Museum of Ethnology.

Fernandez, J.W. 1986. The argument of images and the experience of returning to the whole. In V.W. Turner and E.M. Bruner, eds., *The anthropology of experience*, 159–87. Urbana: University of Illinois Press.

– ed. 1991. *Beyond metaphor: The theory of tropes in anthropology.* Stanford: Stanford University Press.

Ferrara, N. 1990. *Art therapy with a Cree Indian boy.* Masters' thesis. Montpelier: Vermont College of Norwich University.

– 1991. Luke's map of the journey: Art therapy with a Cree Indian boy. *Journal of Child and Youth Care* 6, 73–8.

– 1992. Adolescent narcissism and ego regression: An art therapy case illustration. *Journal of Child and Youth Care* 7, 49–56.

– 1994. Native American experience of healing through art. *Art Therapy Journal of the American Art Therapy Association* 11, 216–17.

– 1996. Art therapy with a Cree bushman. *The Canadian Art Therapy Association Journal* 10, 1–6.

– 1998. Art therapy with a Cree Indian boy. In A.R. Hiscox and A.C. Calisch, eds., *Tapestry of cultural issues in art therapy,* 49–84. London: Jessica Kingsley Publishers.

– 1999. *Emotional expression among Cree Indians: The role of pictorial representations in the assessment of psychological mindedness.* London: Jessica Kingsley Publishers.

– 2000. *Art therapy with the Quebec Cree: Metonymic and synaesthetic associations in patients' artwork.* Paper presented at the 32nd Algonquian Conference in Montreal, Quebec.

Finnegan, R. 1992. *Oral traditions and the verbal arts.* New York: Routledge.

Fisher, R. 1992. *Contact and conflict: Indian-European relations in British Columbia 1774–1890.* Second edition. Vancouver: University of British Columbia Press.

Foucault, M. 1971. *L'ordre du discours.* Paris: Gallimard.

– 1972. *The archaeology of knowledge.* A.M. Sheridan Smith, trans. New York: Pantheon Books.

– 1979. *The history of sexuality, Vol. I: An Introduction.* New York: Random House.

– 1984. On the genealogy of ethics: An overview of work in progress. In P. Rabinow, ed., *The Foucault reader,* 340–72. New York: Pantheon Books.

Francis, D. and T. Morantz. 1983. *Partners in furs: A history of the fur trade in Eastern James Bay 1600–1870.* Montreal: McGill-Queen's University Press.

Frank, J.D. and J.B. Frank. 1991. *Persuasion and healing: A comparative study of psychotherapy.* Third edition. Baltimore: Johns Hopkins University Press.

Franklin, M. 1992. Art therapy and self-esteem. *Art Therapy: Journal of the American Art Therapy Association* 9, 78–84.

Frenette, J. 1985. *The history of the Chibougamau Crees: An Amerindian band reveals its identity.* Chibougamau: Cree Indian Centre of Chibougamau.

Frideres, J.S. 1998. *Aboriginal peoples in Canada*. Fifth edition. Scarborough: Prentice-Hall.

Fulford, G.T. 1994. *Children's drawings in a Mashkeko ('Swampy Cree') community*. Unpublished doctoral dissertation. Hamilton: McMaster University.

– 1998. *An ethnographer's understanding of Algonquian languages and linguistics*. Unpublished manuscript.

– 2000a. *Synaesthetic and metaphoric associations in Swampy Cree language and children's art*. Unpublished manuscript.

– 2000b. Personal communication. Winnipeg: University of Winnipeg.

Geertz, C. 1984. "From the Native's point of view": On the nature of anthropological understanding. In R.A. Shweder and R.A. Levine, eds., *Culture theory*, 123–36. Cambridge: Cambridge University Press.

– 1995. *After the fact. Two countries, four decades, one anthropologist*. Cambridge: Harvard University Press.

Gerhardt, J. and C. Stinson. 1996. The therapeutic encounter: Neutral context or social construction? In D.I. Slobin, J. Gerhardt, A. Kyfratzis, and J. Quguo, eds., *Social interaction, social context, and language: Essays in honor of Susan Ervin-Tripp*, 449–68. Mahwah: Laurence Erlbaum Associates.

Ghostkeeper, E. 1996. *Spirit gifting: The concept of spiritual exchange*. Calgary: The University of Calgary.

Goulet, J.G. 1994a. Ways of knowing: Towards a narrative ethnography of experiences among the Dene Tha. *Journal of Anthropological Research* 50, 113–39.

– 1994b. Reincarnation as a fact of life among contemporary Dene Tha. In A. Mills and R. Slobodin, eds., *Amerindian rebirth: Reincarnation belief among North American Indians and Inuit*, 156–76. Toronto: University of Toronto Press.

Gregory, D. 1989. Traditional Indian healers in northern Manitoba: An emerging relationship with the Health Care System. *Native Studies Review* 5, 163–73.

Gupta, A. and J. Ferguson. 1992. Beyond "culture": Space, identity, and the politics of difference. *Cultural Anthropology* 7, 6–23.

Gusdorf, G. 1980. The conditions and limits of autobiography. In J. Olney, ed., *Autobiography: Essays theoretical and critical*, 28–48. Princeton: Princeton University Press.

Hallowell, A.I. 1955. *Culture and experience*. Philadelphia: University of Pennsylvania Press.

– 1963. Ojibwa world view and disease. In I. Galdston, ed., *Man's image in medicine and anthropology*, 258–315. New York: International Universities Press.

– 1966. The role of dreams in Ojibwa culture. In G.E. von Grunebaum and R. Caillois, eds., *The dream and human societies*, 267–92. Berkeley: University of California Press.

Hawkes, T. 1977. *Structuralism and semiotics*. Berkeley: University of California Press.

Heelas, P. and A. Lock. eds. 1981. *Indigenous psychologies: The anthropology of the self*. London: Academic Press.

Heidegger, M. 1977 Building dwelling thinking. In D.F. Krell, ed., *Martin Heidegger: Basic writings*, 319–39. New York: Harper & Row.

Henriksen, G. 1974. *Hunters in the barrens: The Naskapi on the edge of the white man's world*. St John's: Memorial University of Newfoundland (Newfoundland Social and Economic Studies no. 12).

Hill, J.H. and J.T. Irvine. 1992. *Responsibility and evidence in oral discourse*. London: Cambridge University Press.

Hinton, A.L. 1993. A prolegomenon to a processual approach to the emotions. *Ethos* 21, 417–51.

Hobsbawn, E. 1983. Introduction: Inventing traditions. In E. Hobsbawn and T. Ranger, eds., *The invention of tradition*, 1–14. Cambridge: Cambridge University Press.

Howes, D., ed. 1991. *The varieties of sensory experience*. Toronto: University of Toronto Press.

Ingold, T. 1996. Hunting and gathering as ways of perceiving the environment. In R. Ellen and K. Fukui, eds., *Redefining Nature*, 117–55. Oxford: Berg.

– 1999. On the social relations of the hunter-gatherer band. In R.B. Lee and R. Daly, eds., *The Cambridge Encyclopedia of Hunter-Gatherers*, 399–410. Cambridge: Cambridge University Press.

Irvine, J.T. 1979. Formality and informality in communicative events. *American Anthropologist* 81, 773–90.

– 1982. Language and affect: Some cross-cultural issues. In H. Byrnes, ed., *Contemporary perceptions of language: Interdisciplinary dimensions*, 31–47. Washington: Georgetown University Press.

– 1992. Insult and responsibility: Verbal abuse in a Wolof village. In J.H. Hill and J.T. Irvine, eds., *Responsibility and evidence in oral discourse*, 105–34. London: Cambridge University Press.

Izard, C.E. 1977. *Human emotions*. New York: Plenum Press.

Jackson, M. 1995. *At home in the world*. Durham: Duke University Press.

Jenness, D. 1977. *Indians of Canada*. Seventh edition. Toronto: University of Toronto Press.

Johnson, R.M. 1988. *The transpersonal exploration of unconscious processes through a centering and projective artform*. Doctoral dissertation. Southboro: The Union of Experimenting Colleges.

Keesing, R.M. 1987. Anthropology as interpretive quest. *Current Anthropology* 28, 161–76.

Kerby, P. 1991. *Narrative and the self*. Bloomington: Indiana University Press.

Kirmayer, L.J. 1989. Psychotherapy and the cultural concept of the person. *Santé, Culture, Health* 6, 241–70.

Kirmayer, L.J., K. Gill, C. Fletcher, Y. Ternar, L. Boothroyd, C. Quesney, A. Smith, and N. Ferrara. 1994. *Suicide in Canadian Aboriginal populations: Emerging trends in research and intervention*. Report #1, Prepared for the Royal Commission on Aboriginal Peoples. Montreal: McGill University, Culture and Mental Health Unit, Department of Psychiatry.

Klein, M. 1961. *Narrative of a child analysis*. New York: Free Press.

Knapp, A.B. and W. Ashmore. 1999. Archaeological landscapes: Constructed, conceptualized, ideational. In W. Ashmore and A.B. Knapp, eds., *Archaeologies of landscape*, 1–30. Oxford: Blackwell Publishers.

Knight, R. 1965. A re-examination of hunting, trapping and territoriality among the northeastern Algonkian Indians. In A. Leeds and A. Vayda, eds., *Man, culture and animals: The role of animals in human ecological adjustments*. Washington, D.C.: American Association for the Advancement of Science.

Korovkin, M. and G. Lanoue. 1988. On the substantiality of form: Interpreting symbolic expression in the paradigm of social organization. *Comparative Studies in Society and History* 30, 613–48.

Kramer, E. 1971. *Art as therapy with children*. New York: Schocken Books.

– 1979. *Childhood and art therapy: Notes on theory and application*. New York: Schocken Books.

Lacan, J. 1949. Le stade du miroir comme fondateur de la fonction du Je. *Revue française de psychanalyse* 4.

Lakoff, G. 1987. *Women, fire and dangerous things*. Chicago: University of Chicago Press.

Lakoff, G. and M. Johnson. 1980. *Metaphors we live by*. Chicago: University of Chicago Press.

Langer, S.K. 1942. *Philosophy in a new key: A study in the symbolism of reason, rite, and art*. Cambridge: Harvard University Press.

– 1953. *Feeling and form*. New York: Scribner's.

– 1962. *Philosophical sketches*. Baltimore: Johns Hopkins University Press.

Lanoue, G. 1989. *Images in stone: A theory on interpreting rock art*. Rome: Art Center.

– 1991. Language loss, language gain: Cultural camouflage and social change among the Sekani of Northern British Columbia. *Language in Society* 20, 87–115.

– 1992. *Brothers: The politics of violence among the Sekani of Northern British Columbia*. New York: Berg.

– 1995. Mythical pathways: Explorations in the key of myth. *Igitur* 7, 3–16.

– 1998. Personal communication. Montreal: Université de Montréal.

– 1999. *Human monsters and mythical space among Athapaskan-speaking peoples of Northwest Canada*. Unpublished manuscript.

– 2000. L' espace et sa métaphorisation dans le mythe et dans l'idéologie: Les bandes, les tribus et les états. Comité scientifique pour l'histoire de la culture mondiale (auteur collectif). *Prostranstvo. Pamyat', mysl' (L'espace. Mémoire et pensée)*, 5–51. Moscou: Institut des langues slaves de l'Académie des sciences de la Russie.

– 2001. Metonymy and multiple naming in North American Indian Societies. *Imya: Vnutrennyaya stuktura, semanticeskaya aura konteckst (Le nom: Structure interne, champ semantique, et contexte)*, II: 4–9. Moscou: Institut des langues slaves de l'Académie des sciences de la Russie.

Leach, E. 1976. *Culture and communication: The logic by which symbols are connected*. Cambridge: Cambridge University Press.

Leacock, E. 1954. *The Montagnais "hunting territory" and the fur trade*. American Anthropological Association Memoir no. 78.

Leavitt, J. 1996. Meaning and feeling in the anthropology of emotions. *American Ethnologist* 23, 514–39.

Lefebvre, H. 1991. *The production of space*. D. Nicholson-Smith, trans. Oxford: Blackwell.

Lévi-Strauss, C. 1963. *Structural anthropology*. New York: Basic Books.

– 1966. *The savage mind*. London: Weidenfeld and Nicolson.

Lincoln, B. 1989. *Discourse and the construction of society: Comparative studies of myth, ritual and classification*. New York: Oxford University.

Lock, M. and N. Scheper-Hughes. 1990. A critical-interpretive approach in medical anthropology: Rituals and routines of discipline and dissent. In T.M. Johnson and C.F. Sargent, eds., *Medical anthropology: A handbook of theory and method*, 47–72. New York: Greenwood Press.

Lotman, Y. 1990. *The universe of the mind*. A. Shukman, trans. Bloomington: Indiana University Press.

Luria, A.R. 1968. *The mind of a mnemonist*. L. Solotaroff, trans. New York: Basic Books.

Lutz, C.A. 1988. *Unnatural emotions: Everyday sentiments on a micronesian Atoll and their challenge to Western theory*. Chicago: University of Chicago Press.

Lutz, C. and L. Abu-Lughod. 1990. *Language and politics of emotions*. Cambridge: Harvard University Press.

Lutz, C., and G.M. White. 1986. The anthropology of emotions. *Annual Review of Anthropology* 15, 405–36.

Lyon, M.L. and J.M. Barbalet. 1994. Society's body: Emotion and the "somatization" of social theory. In T.J. Csordas, ed., *Embodiment and experience: The existential ground of culture and self*, 48–66. Cambridge: Cambridge University Press.

Marano, L. 1982. Windigo psychosis: The anatomy of an emicetic confusion. *Current Anthropology* 23, 385–412.

Marcus, G. and M. Fischer, eds. 1986. *Anthropology as cultural critique*. Chicago: University of Chicago Press.

Marks, L.E. 1990. Synaesthasia: Perception and metaphor. In F. Burwick and W. Pape, eds., *Aesthetic illusion*, 20–31. New York: Walter de Gruyter.

Martin, C. 1981. *Keepers of the game: Indian-animal relationships and the fur trade*. Berkeley: University of California Press.

Martin, L.H., H. Gutman, and P.H. Hutton. 1988. *Technologies of the self: A seminar with Michel Foucault*. Amherst: The University of Massachusetts Press.

McFarlane, P. and W. Haimila. 1999. *Ancient land, ancient sky*. Toronto: Alfred A. Knopf.

McGee, R.J. and R.L. Warms, eds. 2000. *Anthropological theory: An introductory history*. Second edition. London: Mayfield Publishing.

McLeod, N. 2000. Plains Cree identity: Borderlands, ambiguous genealogies and narrative irony. *Canadian Journal of Native Studies* 20, 437–54.

Meletinsky, E.M. 1998. *The poetics of myth*. G. Lanoue and A. Sadetsky, trans. New York: Garland Publishing.

Miller, J.R. 1989. *Skyscrapers hide the heavens: A history of Indian-White relations in Canada*. Toronto: University of Toronto Press.

– 1996. *Shingwauk's vision: A history of Native residential schools*. Toronto: University of Toronto Press.

Mills, A. 1986. The meaningful universe: Intersecting forces in Beaver Indian cosmology. *Culture* 4, 81–91.

Moore, H.L. 1986. *Space, text and gender: An anthropological study of the Marakwet of Kenya*. Cambridge: Cambridge University Press.

– 1990. *Paul Ricoeur: Action, meaning and text*. In C. Tilley, ed., *Reading material culture: Structuralism, hermeneutics and post-structuralism*, 85–120. Cambridge: Basil Blackwell.

Moore, P. and A. Wheelock. 1990. *Wolverine myths and visions: Dene traditions from Northern Alberta*. Edmonton: University of Alberta Press.

Morantz, T. 1978. Pratiques religieuses des Cris de la Baie James aux XVIIIe et XIXe siècles (d'après les Européens). *Recherches amérindiennes au Québec* 8, 113–22.

– 1980. *The impact of the fur trade on the 18th and 19th century Algonquian Social Organization: An ethnographic, ethnohistoric study of the Eastern James Bay Cree from 1700–1850*. Doctoral dissertation, Department of Anthropology, University of Toronto.

– 1983. *An ethnohistoric study of Eastern James Bay Cree social organization, 1700–1850*. Canadian Ethnology Service Paper No. 88, National Museum of Man Mercury Series. Ottawa: National Museum of Canada.

– 2002. *The white man's gonna getcha: The colonial challenge to the Crees of Quebec*. Montreal: McGill-Queen's University Press.

Napier, A.D. 1992. *Foreign bodies: Performance, art, and symbolic anthropology.* Berkeley: University of California Press.

Niezen, R. 1993. Power and dignity: The social consequences of hydro-electric development for the James Bay Cree. *Canadian Review of Sociology and Anthropology* 30, 510–29.

– 1997. Healing and conversion: Medical evangelism in James Bay Cree society. *Ethnohistory* 44, 463–91.

– 1998. *Defending the land: Sovereignty and forest life in James Bay Society.* Boston: Allyn and Bacon.

Nuttall, M. 1992. *Arctic homeland*. Toronto: University of Toronto Press.

Ochs, E. and L. Capps. 1996. Narrating the self. *Annual Review of Anthropology* 25, 19–43.

O'Neill, J. 1994. Vico and myth. In M. Danesi and F. Nuessel, eds., *The imaginative basis of thought and culture: Contemporary perspectives on Giambattista Vico*. Toronto: Canadian Scholars' Press.

Parkin, D. 1985. Reason, emotion, and the embodiment of power. In J. Overing, ed., *Reason and morality,* 135–51. London: Tavistock Publications.

Pennebaker, J.W., ed. 1995. *Emotion, disclosure, and health.* Washington, D.C.: American Psychological Association.

Phillips, S.U. 1976. Some sources of cultural variability in the regulation of talk. *Language in Society* 5, 81–95.

Pred, A. 1990. *Making histories and constructing human geographies: The local transformation of practice, power relations, and consciousness.* Boulder: Westview Press.

Preston, R.J. 1976. Reticence and self-expression: A study of style in social relationships. In W. Cowan, ed., *Papers of the 7th Algonquian Conference (1975)*, 450–94. Ottawa: Carleton University Press.

– 1981. East Main Cree. In J. Helm, ed., *Handbook of North American Indian (Volume 6)*, 196–207. Washington: Smithsonian Institution.

– 1982. Towards a general statement on the Eastern Cree structure of knowledge. In W. Cowan, ed., *Papers of the 13th Algonquian Conference*, 299–306. Ottawa: Carleton University.

– 1988. James Bay Cree syncretism: Persistence and replacement. In W. Cowan, ed., *Papers of the 19th Algonquian Conference*, 147–55. Ottawa: Carleton University.

– 1991. Interference and consequences: An East Cree variant of deviance? *Anthropologica* 33, 69–80.

– 2000. Personal communication. Winnipeg: University of Winnipeg.

– 2002. *Cree narrative: Expressing the personal meanings of events*. Second edition. Montreal: McGill-Queen's University Press.

Prince, R. 1993. Psychiatry among the James Bay Cree: A focus on pathological grief reactions. *Transcultural Psychiatric Research Review* 30, 3–50.

Qitsualik, R. 1998. Nunani: Isuma. *Nunatsiaq News*, 13 August, 1998.

Rabinow, P. and W.M. Sullivan, eds. 1979. *Interpretive social science: A reader*. Berkeley: University of California Press.

Rappaport, R.A. 1999. *Ritual and religion in the making of humanity*. Cambridge: Cambridge University Press.

Report of the Cree-Naskapi Commission. 1994. Ottawa: The Cree-Naskapi Commission.

Richardson, B. 1991. *Strangers devour the land*. Vancouver: Douglas & McIntyre.

Riches, D. 1982. *Northern nomadic hunter-gatherers: A humanistic approach*. London: Academic Press.

Ricoeur, P. 1970. *Freud and philosophy: An essay on interpretation*. D. Savage, trans. New Haven: Yale University Press.

– 1984. *Time and narrative, Three Volumes*. K. McLaughlin and D. Pellauer, trans. Chicago: University of Chicago Press.

Ridington, R. 1990. *Little bit know something: Stories in a language of anthropology*. Iowa: University of Iowa Press.

Rogers, E.S. 1963. *The hunting group – hunting territory complex among the Mistassini Indians*. Ottawa: National Museum of Man, Bulletin 195.

Rosaldo, M.Z. 1982. The things we do with words: Ilongot speech acts and speech act theory in philosophy. *Language in Society* 11, 203–37.

– 1984. Toward an anthropology of self and feeling. In R.A. Shweder and R.A. Levine, eds., *Culture theory: Essays on mind, self, and emotion*, 136–57. London: Cambridge University Press.

Rubin, J.A. 1984. *The art of art therapy*. New York: Brunner/Mazel.

Rudnytsky, P.L. 1993. Introduction. In P.L. Rudnytsky, ed., *Transitional objects and potential spaces: Literary uses of D.W. Winnicott*, xi-xxii. New York: Columbia University Press.

Ryan, J. 1992. Eroding Innu cultural tradition: Individualization and communality. *Journal of Canadian Studies* 26, 94–111.

Ryden, K.C. 1993. *Mapping the invisible landscape: Folklore, writing, and the sense of place*. Iowa: University of Iowa Press.

Salisbury, R.F. 1986. *A homeland for the Cree: Regional development in James Bay 1971–81*. Montreal: McGill-Queen's University Press.

Sampson, E.E. 1988. The debate on individualism. *American Psychologist* 43, 15–22.

Sapir, E. 1921. *Language*. New York: Harcourt Brace.

Schafer, R. 1981. Narration in the psychoanalytic dialogue. In W.J.T. Mitchell, ed., *On narrative*, 29–53. Chicago: University of Chicago Press.

Scheper-Hughes, N. and M. Lock. 1987. The mindful body: A prolegomenon to future work in medical anthropology. *Medical Anthropology Quarterly* 1, 6–41.

Scollon, R. and S.B.K. Scollon. 1981. *Narrative, literacy and face in interethnic communication*. Norwood: Ablex.

Scott, C. 1989. Knowledge construction among Cree hunters: Metaphors and literal understanding. *Journal de la Société des Américanistes* 75, 193–208.

– 1996. Science for the west, myth for the rest? In L. Nader, ed., *Naked science: Anthropological inquiry into boundaries, power, and knowledge*, 69–86. New York: Routledge.

Searle, J. 1969. *Speech acts: An essay in the philosophy of language*. London: Cambridge University Press.

Sharp, H.S. 1988. *The transformation of bigfoot: Maleness, power, and belief among the Chipewyan*. Washington: Smithsonian Institution Press.

Sherzer, J. 1987. A discourse-centered approach to language and culture. *American Anthropologist* 89, 295–309.

Shkilnyk, A.M. 1985. *A poison stronger than love: The destruction of an Ojibwa community*. New Haven: Yale University Press.

Shore, B. 1996. *Culture in mind: Cognition, culture, and the problem of meaning*. New York: Oxford University Press.

Shuman, A. 1992. "Get outa my face": Entitlement and authoritative discourse. In J.H. Hill and J.T. Irvine, eds., *Responsibility and evidence in oral discourse*, 135–60. London: Cambridge University Press.

Shweder, R.A. 1990. Cultural psychology: What is it? In J.W. Stigler, R.A. Shweder, and G. Herdt, eds., *Cultural psychology: Essays on comparative human development*, 1–43. New York: Cambridge University Press.

Shweder, R.A. and E.J. Bourne. 1982. Does the concept of the person vary cross-culturally? In A.J. Marsella and G.M. White, eds., *Cultural conceptions of mental health and therapy*, 97–137. Dordrecht: D. Reidel.

Smith, D.M. 1973. *Inkonze: Magico-religious beliefs of contact-traditional Chipewyan trading at Fort Resolution, NWT, Canada*. Ottawa: National Museum of Man.

Sökefeld, M. 1999. Debating self, identity and culture in anthropology. *Current Anthropology* 40, 417–47.

Speck, F.G. 1977. *Naskapi: The savage hunters of the Labrador peninsula*. Norman: University of Oklahoma Press.

Spielmann, R. 1998. *"You're so fat!": Exploring Ojibwe discourse*. Toronto: University of Toronto Press.

Spiro, M.E. 1993. Is the Western conception of the self "peculiar" within the context of the world cultures? *Ethos* 21, 107–53.

Stairs, A. 1992. Self-image, world-image: Speculations on identity from experiences with Inuit. *Ethos* 20, 116–26.

Storm, H. 1972. *Seven arrows*. New York: Ballantine Books.

Strathern, M. 1987. The limits of auto-anthropology. In A. Jackson, ed., *Anthropology at Home*, 16–37. London: Tavistock Publications.

Tanner, A. 1979. *Bringing home animals: Religious ideology and mode of production of the Mistassini Cree hunters*. St John's: Memorial University of Newfoundland.

– 1997. Personal communication. Montreal, Quebec.

– 1999. Culture, social change, and Cree opposition to the James Bay hydroelectric development. In James F. Hornig, ed., *Social and environmental impacts of the James Bay hydroelectric project*, 121–140. Montreal: McGill-Queen's University Press.

Tanner, A. 2000. Personal communication. St John's, Newfoundland.

Tarasoff, K.J. 1980. *Persistent ceremonialism: The Plains Cree and Saulteaux*. Canadian Ethnology Service Paper No. 69, National Museum of Man Mercury Series. Ottawa: National Museum of Canada.

Taussig, M. 1993. *Mimesis and alterity: A particular history of the senses*. New York: Routledge.

Thornton, T.F. 1997. Anthropological studies of Native American place naming. *American Indian Quarterly* 21, 209–28.

Tilley, C. 1999. *Metaphor and material culture*. Oxford: Blackwell Publishers.

Tooker, E. and W.C. Sturtevant. 1979. Native North American spirituality of Eastern Woodlands. New York: Paulist Press.

Trigger, B.G. 1985. *Natives and newcomers: Canada's "Heroic Age" reconsidered*. Montreal: McGill-Queen's University Press.

Trott, C.G. 1982. The Inuk as object: Some problems in the study of Inuit social organization. *Etudes/Inuit/Studies* 6, 93–108.

Tuan, Y.F. 1975. Place: An experiential perspective. *Geographical Review* 65, 151–65.

– 1977. *Space and place: The perspective of experience.* Minneapolis: University of Minnesota Press.

– 1991. Language and the making of place: A narrative-descriptive approach. *Annals of the Association of American Geographers* 81, 684–96.

– 1993. *Passing strange and wonderful: Aesthetics, nature and culture.* New York: Kodansha.

Turner, B.S. 1984. *The body and society: Explorations in social theory.* Oxford: Basil Blackwell.

Turner, D.H. 1978. Ideology and elementary structures. *Anthropologica* 20, 223–47.

– 1979. Behind the myths. In D.H. Turner and G.A. Smith, eds., *Challenging anthropology,* 117–36. Toronto: McGraw-Hill Ryerson.

Turner, D.H. and P. Wertman. 1977. *Shamattawa: The structure of social relations in a Northern Algonkian Band.* (Canadian Ethnology Service paper No. 36. Ottawa: National Museum of Canada.

Turner, T. 1995. Social body and embodied subject: Bodiliness, subjectivity and sociality among the Kayapo. *Cultural Anthropology* 10, 143–70.

Turner, V. 1965. Ritual symbolism, morality, and social structure among the Ndembu. In M. Fortes and G. Dieterlen, eds., *African systems of thought,* 48–58. London: Oxford University Press.

– 1967. *The forest of symbols: Aspects of Ndembu Ritual.* Ithaca: Cornell University Press.

– 1969. *The ritual process.* Chicago: Aldine.

– 1973. Symbols in African ritual. *Science* 179, 1100–5.

– 1974. *Dramas, fields, and metaphors: Symbolic action in human society.* Ithaca: Cornell University Press.

– 1979. Betwixt and between: The liminal period in *rites de passage.* In W.A. Lessa and E.Z. Vogt, eds., *Reader in comparative religion,* fourth edition, 234–43. New York: Harper & Row.

– 1981. Social dramas and stories about them. In W.J.T. Mitchell, ed., *On narrative,* 141–68. Chicago: University of Chicago Press.

Ulman, E. and P. Dachinger. 1975. *Art therapy: In theory and practice.* New York: Schocken Books.

van Gennep, A. 1909. *The rites of passage.* M.B. Vizedom and G.L. Caffee, trans. London: Routledge & Kegan Paul.

Waldram, J.B. 1988. *As long as the rivers run: Hydroelectric development and Native communities in Western Canada*. Winnipeg: University of Manitoba Press.

– 1990. Access to traditional medicine in a Western Canadian city. *Medical Anthropology* 12, 325–48.

Waldram, J.B., D.A. Herring, and T.K. Young. 1995. *Aboriginal health in Canada*. Toronto: University of Toronto Press.

Warner, J.A. 1978. Contemporary Algonkian legend painting. *American Indian Art Magazine* 3, 58–78.

Wheeler, R.H. 1920. *The synaesthasia of a blind subject*. University of Oregon Publications I.

Wheeler, R.H. and T.D. Cutsforth. 1922. Synaesthasia and meaning. *American Journal of Psychology* 33, 218–368.

White, M. and D. Epstein. 1990. *Narrative means to therapeutic ends*. New York: W.W. Norton and Company.

Whittaker, E. 1992. The birth of the anthropological self and its career. *Ethos* 20, 191–219.

Wikan, U. 1990. *Managing turbulent hearts*. Chicago: The University of Chicago Press.

– 1991. Toward an experience-near anthropology. *Cultural Anthropology* 6, 285–305.

Wilson, L. 1979. Introduction: Kramer's theoretical formulations. In E. Kramer, *Childhood and art therapy: Notes on theory and application*, xxvii-xxxiv. New York: Schocken Books.

Winnicott, D.W. 1949. Mind and its relation to the psyche-soma. In D.W. Winnicott, *Collected Papers: Through paediatrics to psycho-analysis*. London: Tavistock Publications.

– 1971. *Playing and reality*. London: Routledge.

Yates, F.A. 1966. *The art of memory*. London: Routledge & Kegan Paul.

Young, D., G. Ingram, and L. Swartz. 1989. *Cry of the eagle: Encounters with a Cree healer*. Toronto: University of Toronto Press.

Index

Abenaki, 7, 139n3
Aboriginal Healing Foundation, 39
aboriginality, 39, 40
Aboriginal Wellness Gathering, 39
accommodation, 32, 45
acculturation, 15, 20, 59, 130, 139n16, 145n3
acculturative stress, 41
alcohol abuse, 17, 20, 22, 39, 52, 56, 82
alexithymia, 36
Algonquian, 139n5, 141n6
alterity, 126
ancestral spirits, 72
animal-doctor relationships, 12, 43–4, 65–6, 68, 70–1, 73–5, 112, 122, 145n7
animism, 137n6
anthropology, 9, 24–5, 118, 127, 129–31, 136n7, 138n8
Apache, 48, 116, 145n26
artist, 95, 105, 114, 129
art-making, 7, 8, 92, 98, 105, 109, 115–16, 123, 133, 146n8
art psychotherapy. *See* art therapy
art therapy, 3, 4, 7, 8, 11–13, 35, 50, 57, 64, 75–7, 78, 81, 85, 89, 92–3, 96–8, 100–3, 105–9, 111–12, 114–26, 128–30, 134, 143nn4, 11, 144nn15, 21, 145n2; diagnostic procedures in, 4, 93, 132, 142n2
artwork, 10, 12, 68, 78, 81–2, 92–3, 95, 98–9, 101–2, 104–5, 109, 112, 114–15, 117, 128–9, 136n10, 141n13, 143nn4, 11
Assembly of First Nations, 40
assimilation, 31, 138n9
atemporality, 107
Athapaskan, 48
autobiography, 143n5

Band Council, 19, 21–2, 40
Bedouin, 145n6
being alive well, 17
betwixt and between phase, 112
biomedicine, 31
brotherhood, 24–5, 40, 137n5
bush, 3, 11–12, 17–20, 22–3, 26, 28, 30–4, 38, 46, 57, 62, 64, 67, 71–4, 76–7, 80, 82, 104–9, 111–14, 120, 123–4, 126, 130, 140n13, 141nn4, 8, 142n2, 144nn15, 20, 145n3
bushcamp, 18, 24, 33, 66, 71–2, 76

bush consciousness, 61
bush economy, 26
bushman, 56, 72, 140n13

Cartesian debate, 52
Christianity, 16, 20–1, 32, 45
clinical assessment, 3–4
clinician, 10, 100, 127–9
cognitive style, 124, 131, 146n8; field dependent, 124; field independent, 124, 146n8
collectivity, 9, 11, 14, 36–7, 39–41, 44, 61–2, 66, 78, 83, 125, 127, 130, 138n8
colonialism, 9, 11–12, 36, 44, 51, 136n9
colonial mentality, 39
composite self, 3, 14, 38, 42, 44, 78, 108, 112, 122, 124–5, 130, 133
condensation, 101
creative art process, 3, 99
cross-modal shifts, 85
cultural brokerage, 44–5, 139n16
cultural pluralism, 20
cultural repression, 9

decolonization, 128
defense mechanisms, 140n12
deflective responses, 51
depression, 22
dialogic exchange, 14, 93, 99, 113–14, 118, 130, 132
discourse, 9, 11–12, 40, 46–7, 50–1, 59, 61, 64–6, 75–6, 78–80, 92–3, 101, 109, 112, 118–19, 121–2, 124–5, 138n14, 145nn6, 7
discursive practice, 12, 46, 93, 120, 136n10
discursive space, 15
dreams, 43, 68–71, 76, 86

ecocentrism, 42, 61
ecosystem, 64
egocentrism, 23–4, 42–3, 45
elders, 8, 13, 17, 24, 28–9, 38, 41, 45, 57, 65, 71, 79, 91, 111, 128–9, 131, 133–4
embodied sociality, 140n11
embodied thoughts, 52
embodiment, 55, 70, 72, 83, 86, 88
emotional expression, 34, 36, 52, 54–5, 142n2
emotional health. *See* health
emotions, 4, 7, 12, 45, 52–3, 71, 84, 105, 130, 139n7, 139n8
emotivity, 7
emplaced experience, 144n18
ethnography, 8–10, 12–14, 47, 100, 126, 128–30, 135n5, 145n6
ethnoprofile, 14–15, 17–18, 31, 33–4
ethno-psychology, 10
experiential knowledge, 120

fishing, 22, 27–8, 33
folklore, 123
folktales, 65, 79
fur-trade, 21, 23–5, 27–32, 138n8

gestalt perception, 84
goose break, 19, 108

habitus, 121, 140n11, 145n5
healer, 56–7, 128–30, 136n2, 140n14
healing, 3, 8–9, 11, 13, 39, 51, 56–7, 59, 97, 103, 105, 120–1, 123, 133–4, 140n15, 144n13
health, 7–8; emotional 8; mental 3, 8, 12, 54 ; physical 8; spiritual 8, 18
hearing impairment, 3–4, 104, 126, 131
hierarchy, 49, 53, 72–3, 75, 113, 141n9
holding environment, 105

household, 25
Hudson Bay, 14, 30
Hudson's Bay Company, 16, 23, 28, 30, 32
human relationships, 11, 55
hunter-gatherer, 81, 114–15, 140n1, 146n8
hunting, 15, 17–19, 21–4, 26–9, 32–3, 35, 38, 41, 48, 54, 56–7, 64, 66–7, 70–2, 80, 109, 113, 137n5, 140n15
hydro-electric project, 24, 33–4, 38–9, 91
hyperactivity, 4, 104

iconic production, 7, 12, 79, 84, 141n11
identity, 4, 8–9, 14, 35–8, 50, 52, 64, 67, 76, 91, 111, 118–19, 123–4, 126, 129, 136n8, 140n10, 140n2
ideological communitas, 45
Ilongot, 50
image, 3, 7, 9–10, 12, 37, 40, 63, 68–9, 73–5, 78–80, 83, 85–6, 95, 105, 113, 120, 123, 128, 139n6, 142nn1, 4
image acts, 47, 78–9, 141n11
image schemas, 84
imagined communities, 11, 36–7, 40, 136n8
Income Security Program, 22–3, 34
indirection, 49–51
individual autonomy, 3, 48, 61
individualism, 10, 23, 25, 42, 45, 54, 113, 138n15, 139n15
individuality, 41, 43, 51, 54, 61, 124, 127
individuation, 11, 97, 101, 122
intentional world, 115, 144n23
interaction patterns, 47–8, 51, 59
interagentivity, 115–17
interanimation, 116–17
interpersonal relationships, 49
Inuit, 7, 9, 33, 139n3, 140n2
inventing traditions, 145n2

James Bay, 11, 14–16, 25, 27–9, 33, 38

kinesics, 47, 139n1
kinship, 24–5, 55, 137n4, 137n5

language, 20, 31, 38, 41, 45, 47, 52, 60, 67, 94, 113, 120
learned helplessness, 41
legend, 65
lexicon, 141n14, 145n25
liminality, 102, 106, 112, 114, 144n14
liminal phase, 100, 102–3, 107, 111–12, 114, 119
liminoidal phase, 100–1

medical pluralism, 17, 121
medicine bag, 17
medicine wheel, 101–2, 144nn12, 13
memoryscape, 91, 142n1
mental health. *See* health
mental space. *See* space
meta-narrative, 77
metaphor, 12, 60, 63, 65, 79–81, 83, 90–1, 113–15, 121, 137n5, 141n11, 142n17, 144n16
metonymy, 11, 12, 60, 63, 65, 70, 75, 80–1, 83, 88, 91, 101, 107, 112, 114, 117, 119–21, 123–4, 142n17, 144n15
mimesis, 126
missionaries, 16–17, 21, 31, 141n14
mnemonic techniques, 142n1
Mohawk, 7, 139n3
moose break, 19, 108

moral landscape, 145n26
multisensorial experience, 131
multivocality, 101
Mursi, 50
myth, 12, 36, 46, 59–65, 68, 74, 76, 107, 112, 123, 128, 136n12, 140n3
mythic space. *See* space
mythological knowledge, 62–4, 75, 119, 121, 123
mythopoesis, 12, 46, 50, 63, 83, 88, 121
mythopoetic thought, 11–12, 59–60, 64, 69, 78–9, 88–9, 107, 109, 118–21, 130, 134

narrative, 3, 7, 10–13, 16, 34, 36, 47, 59, 61, 64–5, 68, 74, 75–80, 91–3, 95, 100–2, 107, 109, 113, 118, 119–20, 122, 124, 126, 128, 130, 135n4, 136n13, 141n12, 142n3
narrative discourse. *See* discourse
nature-nurture debate, 52
neuroses, 54
non-human personhood, 46, 113, 125, 144n24
non-interference, 48
Northern Quebec Agreement, 33

obviation, 139n5
Ojibwa, 7, 9–10, 39, 43, 139nn3, 5, 141n6, 144n24
oral tradition, 38

pan-Indianism, 39–40, 138n14, 144n12
patient-centred approach, 13, 126
patrilineal society, 24
Pentecostalism, 16–17
personality types, 135n6
personhood, 64, 70
pharmacopoeia, 17, 32
physical health. *See* health
physical space. *See* space
place, 11–12, 90–2, 95, 97–8, 108, 114–16, 118–19, 123, 142n1, 144n22
poetic wisdom, 140n3
postliminal phase, 100
preliminal phase, 100
production of space, 89
psychiatry, 3–4, 54, 114, 129
psychoanalysis, 97, 105, 122, 142n4, 143nn7, 10
psychology, 9, 84
psychosis, 69
psychotherapeutic approaches, 100
psychotherapy, 3, 7, 54, 95, 97, 121–2, 126, 143nn6, 7

reciprocity, 68, 70, 77
residential school, 31, 138n9
residential treatment, 3, 4, 71, 77, 82, 84, 102, 105, 126
resistance, 41
reticence, 49, 52–3
revitalization, 41
rite of passage, 26, 100
ritual, 12, 17, 19, 26, 57, 60, 64–6, 70, 76–7, 89, 97, 101, 103, 105, 107, 111–12, 118–19, 123, 130, 143nn7, 8, 11, 144n14
ritualized space, 11, 89, 93, 95, 97, 100
Rock Crees, 141n5

Saulteaux, 39
schema transformation, 84, 123
Scored Archetypal Test (SAT9), 36
Second World War, 30, 34
sedenterization, 15
self, 3, 7, 9–13, 26, 36, 37–9, 42, 44–6, 51–

2, 54–7, 59, 61, 64, 66, 69–70, 77–8, 80–1, 83, 89–91, 93, 97, 100, 103–7, 112–13, 117–21, 123–8, 130–1, 138n12, 139n15, 140n9, 143n4, 144n22
self-awareness, 93, 95, 97, 128, 136n13
self-discovery, 102, 123, 128
self-expression, 8, 49, 123, 135n4
self-government, 33, 138n10
self-in-nature, 3, 10, 38, 62, 70, 78, 100, 118
self-in-the-collectivity, 3, 10, 38, 44, 62, 78, 100, 118, 120
self-reflection, 4, 92–4, 97, 99, 101, 105–6, 109, 111–12, 119, 122, 124, 130, 142n3
self-representation, 145n4
self-transformation, 102, 105–7, 125
sexual abuse, 52
shaman, 16, 18, 27, 51, 69, 143n7
Shamattawa Crees, 56, 137n5
sign language, 82, 85
silence, 7, 47, 48, 51, 53, 66, 112, 118
social organization, 24–5, 27, 55, 137n4, 138n8
social pathology, 41
social space. *See* space
sociocentrism, 42, 54, 61, 138n15
somatization, 54, 139n8
sorcery, 70
space, 8, 13, 27, 50, 57, 68, 74, 89–91, 93, 95, 97–9, 103, 105–7, 111–12, 115, 117, 119–20, 123–4, 127, 129–30, 133, 144n22; mental, 92, 96, 115–16; mythic, 111; physical 12, 92, 96; social, 38, 92, 96
spatial schema, 89
speech acts, 47, 49, 78–9, 139n4
spiritual health. *See* health
stories, 8, 38, 63, 76, 79, 108, 119–20, 128, 142n1
storytelling, 12, 79, 128, 131, 136n11
subsistence, 25
substance abuse, 44
suicide, 20, 39, 44, 52, 71, 141n8
sweat lodges, 18, 57, 140n15
syllabics, 83–4, 124, 141n14
symbols, 5, 16, 41–3, 45, 57, 60, 63, 83, 97, 101, 105, 112, 120, 143n11, 144nn12, 13, 145n7
synaesthasia, 12, 83–4, 86, 88, 124, 131, 141nn15, 16
syncretism, 16–17, 121

taciturnity, 49, 52–3
teacher, 4, 20, 129
technique of the self, 93
technologies of power, 45–6
theory of practice, 90
therapist, 129
transitional space, 106
trapping, 22, 41, 137n5
treaty, 138n10

Ulman Personality Assessment Procedure (UPAP), 142n2

violence, 20, 39

walking-out ceremony, 26
Wechuge, 69
Whiskey-jack, 65
wigwam, 15–16, 18–19, 26, 57, 66, 76, 91, 109, 140n15
Windigo, 68–9